40 THINGS I LEARNT BY 40

Olaolu Faj Opebiyi

Tobi, Seun, Folakemi, Mide & Dimeji,
The Lessons of life are key
treasures that will follow you
all your days. Keep learning
and God will crown all your
efforts with success

Lashi
Oct '17

info@olaolufajopebiyi.com
www.olaolufajopebiyi.com

FAJ Publishing
London
United Kingdon

"LEARNING IS A TREASURE THAT WILL
FOLLOW ITS OWNER EVERYWHERE"

- CHINESE PROVERB

CONTENTS

PREFACE

In 2014, as I was turning 40, I decided to write what I had learnt over my few years of existence and share one lesson with my closest friends for each of the 40 days leading up to my 40th birthday. I received a lot of good feedback from my friends and was encouraged to publish this and share it with the world.

For a couple of years I did nothing with it until the 26th of February 2016, whilst on my way to a work assignment in Amsterdam, something I would never have imagined in my wildest dreams happened to me.

It was an early morning flight from London Luton airport and as I sat down on my seat waiting to take off on an Easyjet aircraft, I sent a message on my phone to a friend of mine about a prayer. Little did I know that the man sitting beside me was looking over my shoulders. He got up a few minutes later saying he was going to the bathroom. The next thing I knew two armed police officers appeared at my seat asking me to hand over my phone and get off the plane!

I was apparently considered a threat and escorted off the plane for questioning. The Police discovered I was a Christian and after about 10 minutes of checks, they radioed the pilot to say they did not see any reason to prevent me from flying. The pilot still refused to let me back on the plane and I had to catch another flight about 4 hours later. (See the full account of my story on the Guardian website: http://www.theguardian.com/uk-news/2016/mar/03/man-removed-easyjet-flight-luton-prayer-message-phone)

This experience became one of those significant moments in one's life that makes everything you have been through flash before your eyes and you begin to ask some hard questions.

What if I became irate and outraged for being apprehended for something I had not been guilty of? What if the officer got up on the wrong side of the bed? What if I was detained at my destination in a strange country? How can people that don't know you instantly judge you without having concrete proof of any wrongdoing? Why have we become so afraid?

Since the incident, I have been invited to quite a few radio interviews and one of the questions that I have always been asked is "How were you able to stay so calm in that situation?"

That's easy, as I have learnt quite a few things over the last few decades of my life to help me put things into perspective and respond to the situations that unexpectedly come my way.

This experience revived my desire to share the things I have learnt in the hope that it will help someone else who is seeking some sense in this sometimes challenging arena called life.

INTRODUCTION

As I approach my 40th year, I am doing a lot of thinking and soul searching and as each day goes by certain lessons ring out loud and clear in my mind. I really don't have any great achievements to boast about and maybe I shouldn't have considering that I overlooked one very important question, "Where will I be when I am 40?"

I woke up one morning about three years ago and analysed my life – newly married, a baby on the way, a job taking me nowhere fast and a bank balance in deficit of £200 or thereabouts. That had been the status for over a year; I became extremely restless and I knew this was definitely where I did not want to be.

It dawned on me that 40 was around the corner and I was nowhere near the big dream of being a millionaire by 40 – mind you I never had that dream to start with. If one does not aim to get somewhere, it's likely that they will settle for anywhere. It seemed like there were too many wasted years behind me and I scoured my past to find something to justify my existence. Thankfully I did! What I found were lessons, some I had learned, others that were forgotten and those I had been lethargic to act upon.

Long gone were the years when lessons were in classrooms and I had a teacher standing over my shoulder demanding I hand in my assignments. The harsh reality is that the most important lessons to help one succeed are not at all found in the institutions of academia, but in the classroom of life.

My reflections caused me to change my attitude and outlook taking very deliberate actions to embrace the change I wanted. Three years later, with a job earning over 3 times my previous salary, my own house, fulfilment of some personal goals and another baby on the way, I am in a much better place for which I am thankful. I only have about 40 days to mark my 40th year and it does not look likely that I will hit the million pound target - unless I win the lottery or something.

My simple consolation is in the saying "life begins at 40". This time I am hitting the ground running. I am setting my targets; I am putting into practice the lessons I have learned, so watch out for 50 because it will be a very different story.

"For I know the thoughts that I think toward you, says the Lord, thoughts of peace and not of evil, to give you a future and a hope." Jeremiah 29:11

JOGA BONITA

"Life is really simple but we insist on making it complicated" – **Confucius**

"Life is like a game," they say. Such statements almost seem to trivialize the magnitude of the reverence that we place upon this thing called life. After all, life is very serious business. I have always disliked that statement and would stop short of being offended when I heard it said; but the more I experience life, I am forced to affirm that this saying is true, "life is like a game". It is NOT a game because unlike Super Mario you don't have three lives and one extra for being good. This however does not negate it's likeness to a game.

I have observed how things always seem to occur in cycles and how everyone seems to go through some kind of challenge at a very comparable season on their journey through life. I have seen opportunity knock and how it was wooed or repelled by those it sought. I have sat with rich men and observed the manner in which they dealt with people and circumstances that came their way. I have closely rubbed shoulders with the poor and noted how they reacted to situations that they found themselves in.

In all this, I could see a pattern and it almost seemed to me like there was a secret script that was being followed and acted out by different categories of people. This made me conclude that life must really be like a game as everyone seemed to be playing by a set of rules they knew about, or maybe they just merely followed in the steps of others they saw playing the game.

Most of us have learned life merely by observing and copying the people that were examples to us. This reminds me of the story of the lady who would always cut off the ends of her spare ribs, throw them away and then place the main piece in the oven to grill it. Her husband then asked her one day, "Honey, why do you throw away one part of the ribs? They seem perfectly fine to me". She answered, "I don't know, my mother always made hers that way". They then decided to ask her Mom why she made her ribs that way. She replied, "I don't know, my mother used to make them that way". They eventually met up with Grandma and asked the same question to which Grandma replied, "When I got my first oven many years ago, there wasn't enough space to fit in the width of the ribs, so I had to cut off the ends of it and get rid of the other bits".

It is so important that our understanding of life is not only caught by what we have observed, but we should be taught by those we have observed. Sometimes what people call a 'curse' or 'bad luck' - typified by the constant failure in one's endeavours - is not a bad omen cast upon them; but instead could be the result of unproductive and non-progressive behaviour patterns observed from those who nurtured them, who also learnt the same from those who nurtured them, and so on and so forth going down their ancestral line.

If life is like a game, then that means there must be a set of rules by which this game should be played such that we get the best out of it and perhaps even become winners. All games have many things in common and if you understand the principles of playing one game, it would make it easier for you to understand the principles that govern every other game.

A few things that are common to games are:

1. The Aim of the Game (Purpose)

2. The Rules

3. The Enforcers of the Rules (Umpires)

4. The Tools and Techniques of the Game

5. The Players

6. The Scores

7. The Supporters or Fans

8. The Opponents

I have learnt to apply these principles to better understand my journey through life. I will share my perspectives on the above in the days to come.

Joga Bonita is Portuguese for Play Beautifully

JOGA BONITA 2

"On certain continents poverty is more spiritual than material, a poverty that consists of loneliness, discouragement and the lack of meaning in life."
– Mother Teresa

To illustrate the principles that govern games I will use football (soccer) as an example as it is quite common.

THE AIM (PURPOSE): For those of you that do not know anything about football, here is a really simple summary of what it entails. You have 2 teams on opposing sides of a rectangular playing field with 11 players on each side. Using their feet, the aim is to put a round, leather ball in the goal of the opposing team more times than the other team can place the ball in their opponent's goal in order to win the game. This is meant to ensue in a 90-minute time window.

My summary of the purpose of this game may be quite accurate, yet it does not convey a clear understanding to the one who has had no prior knowledge of the game. The background information is vital in trying to make the aim clear. Things like the dimensions of the field of play, the markings on it, the net covering the back of the goal posts, the function of the individual players etc. are tightly connected to how one understands the purpose of the game.

If life is like a game then, what is its aim? I am not sure I can answer that for you, but maybe if you found out a lot more about the playing field - things that make up life - you might get a clearer picture. Things like your mind – how you reason; your will – why you make decisions; and your emotions – how you are feeling, love, hate, fear, anger and so on. What of people? Family, friends, community and your relationship to them? What of the environment around you? How much time do you have? I guess you get the picture.

Philosophers from all types of persuasions tell us there are questions we must ask about life, but they don't quite agree on how many. Some say 6, others say 20 and yet more say 100. Whether you ask 6 or 100 questions, it does not matter as long as you get answers that help you understand life and its purpose. Surely there is someone somewhere who knows something about it! Humans have achieved such great things in the last one thousand years that I refuse to believe that no one has cracked the code on 'The meaning of life'.

The aim of any game is so important that once you lose sight of it your contribution to the game, and your derived benefit from it may pale into futility.

This reminds me of a story an elderly friend of mine told me years ago. When he was a boy, his uncle, a typical Igbo man (a tribe of West African origin), told him this proverb to persuade him to espouse the virtues of teamwork. He said, "When 3 boys urinate on the same spot at the back of the farm, it generates more froth than when one boy urinates alone". My friend thought about the sense to be derived from this parable, but then he had to ask his uncle, "So what do we do with all the froth that we have generated?"

There are various pressures that come from family, friends and community which push us to achieve more; "Be the top of your class", " Pursue qualifications in one of the respectable professions", "Get a well-paying job", "Get married", "Have children", "Buy or build a house", and the list goes on. After generating all this froth, I wonder what next?

I have learnt that I should not go through the motions of what others before me have done or are doing, but to take a step back and ask, think and be sure I understand the aim of this game of life and how I fit into it. Purpose makes the game more beautiful; the collective purpose and my individual place in it.

In conclusion, King Solomon is said to have been one of the wisest kings that lived so maybe a good place to start the quest for the aim of the game can be found in his writings and those of many others. After all, I would not want to spend all my time reinventing the wheel when someone else may already have the answer.

Check out the book of Proverbs and Ecclesiastes in the Bible to find out more about what Solomon said.

JOGA BONITA 3

"We learned about honesty and integrity - that the truth matters... that you don't take shortcuts or play by your own set of rules... and success doesn't count unless you earn it fair and square." – **Michelle Obama**

THE RULES: *Now there are some rules to the game of football (soccer). For instance, only one player (Goalkeeper) on each side is allowed to handle the ball in a designated area, but all the other players must use their feet.*

People say that life is not fair, but I beg to disagree because the issue is that sometimes we are not playing by the rules. Imagine if a player who is not the goalkeeper decides he wants to handle the ball – of course he will get penalised and probably sent off the game.

The thing that I find unfair about life is that it penalises us for breaking the rules even when we are ignorant of them, but then this is not really life's fault, but the error of the one who should have taught us the rules. Sadly ignorance is no excuse and definitely not bliss.

There are rules that must be followed in life, and by virtue of the family we have been born into and the location of our birth, we are naturally subscribed to obey those rules. We may refer to them by different names like family values, traditions, culture, laws of the land, company policy, code of ethics and even religion but they are all rules. Some are unspoken and you are expected to notice them and align, while others are written down and it would take a wise teacher to help you to understand them.

I can't talk about the rules without mentioning the coach. The word was first used as a slang to describe a tutor who carries the student through examinations. Which is why it is also used to describe a vehicle that transports people. A coach is a guide, a teacher, a mentor, a godfather – they know the game reasonably well but are also experts on the rules of the game. A good coach may not necessarily be the best player, but they do know how to get you to play your best game.

When you are young, you usually don't have a choice on who your coach will be. The first coaches we encounter in the game are our parents, so whether good or bad, we are stuck with them for the early years of our lives. At an age of accountability however, you must take responsibility for your actions and you can't blame your coaches for your failures. Great sports men go through a phase where they change their coach, as one coach is better in bringing out certain skills than another.

I have learnt that whatever the endeavour I plan to embark on, there are rules for it. There are also coaches that know how to help me understand and apply those rules to be a winner in my endeavours and I can choose who that good coach will be.

THE ENFORCER OF RULES: *You have four officials who watch the game to check that everyone is playing according to the rules; to punish those who break rules, and to reward those who score goals in line with the rules. Of the four officials, one is actively involved in the game running where the players run. Two are on the sidelines following closely what is happening, and the fourth official stands outside the field of play observing the game.*

No one seems to like the enforcers but they are so necessary to ensure that the game does not descend into chaos. If there were no consequences for breaking rules, most people would not keep them. The enforcers are there to serve the punishments, but more importantly to properly award the rewards of the game. The referee – one to whom something is referred to, upholds the rules.

Different cultures reveal that they have enforcers involved in the day to day activities of their people, the likes of teachers, bosses, traffic wardens, the police, and judges to name a few. But most seem to believe that there is someone silent and invisible watching from the side lines that kind of makes sure that everyone gets their just punishment or reward.

My early experiences with enforcers were not great and I had a strong attitude of rebellion towards them because I only perceived them to be bearers of punishment – especially those who I believed were abusing their power. My rebellion mostly manifested itself in mistrust and avoidance of these figures rather than in open defiance against them. Enforcers are not all bad, for they are the ones responsible for certifying your life's credentials. It may be a certificate or diploma from an institution of learning. It may be a license to practice some profession or trade. It may be a word of commendation affirming your ability and integrity. However they give it, you need to get it so that your game yields the dividends of rewards.

I have since changed my mind-set so that I see the enforcer's prime role as an enabler of the game and not a deterrent to it. They, after all do have the more important job of declaring the winners of the game.

I have been to interviews for jobs, passports, licenses etc. and no matter how impressed the panel was with me; they always sought the opinion of a referee (past teachers, bosses and sometimes even the police). If I continued in my rebellion and avoidance of them, they would not have spoken for me when I needed to get the award that I was due.

As much as the coach knows the rules and trains you to use them, it is the approval of the enforcer that counts. The referee certifies you as a truly beautiful player – a winner.

JOGA BONITA 4

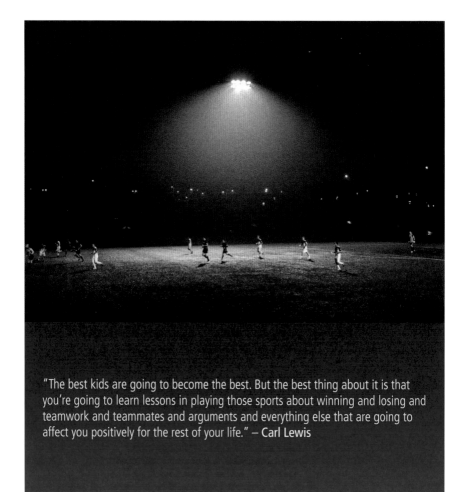

"The best kids are going to become the best. But the best thing about it is that you're going to learn lessons in playing those sports about winning and losing and teamwork and teammates and arguments and everything else that are going to affect you positively for the rest of your life." – **Carl Lewis**

THE TOOLS & TECHNIQUES: the tools would include the football, football boots, shin guards, sportswear, hands, legs, head and more. Techniques include possession play, man marking, zonal defence etc.

A tool is anything that is used as a means of accomplishing a task, while a technique is a method of performance. The technique of the game is not the same as the rules of the game; it is however the way an individual applies the rules to achieve his aim in the game. Tools and techniques are constantly honed on the training ground under the tutelage of the coach. Most players will have a uniform set of tools to work with, however it is the technique that differentiates one player from another, and one team from another.

The minimum expectation of a player is to master his tool – we all have 24 hours in a day, one head, one brain, most have hands and feet etc. What do you do with yours? Many people have a tennis racket and nothing to show for it, but Roger Federer has made over £48 million from his. Everyone can talk and have probably been able to use their gift of the gab to get out of a bad situation or negotiate a free meal, yet Donald Trump gets paid about £1million for talking for an hour.

If I describe a football team that is efficient, clinical and indefatigable in their game you may think Germany. How about a team that is skilful, passionate and sometimes employs the hand of God? Argentina I believe. What of a team that is entertaining, plays effortlessly and with lots of flair? Brazil, Brazil! They've got 'Joga Bonita'.

You may never get noticed for your tools because over 6 billion people have similar. It is the technique that you use that defines who you are, that differentiates you, that gets you noticed and makes you a winner.

I have learnt that it's not what you have (tools), but how you use it (techniques) that counts. When it looks like the rules or the tools are not in your favour, your application of technique can transform that disadvantage into an advantage. A great technique to have in the game of life is a positive attitude.

THE PLAYERS: 11 individuals on each side and several others waiting on the bench.

As much as each person is an individual and has a very significant part to play, the best results in a game are achieved when the individuals play as a team. The saying is true "no man is an island". We are surrounded by people and it is imperative that our ability to interact with others is well developed through the various seasons of our lives.

When people come together for a common purpose, they can achieve results that no individual could accomplish alone. Working with others and creating opportunities for increased cooperation makes greater things possible in our lives and in the world. Sometimes I need to take a break and let another take my place so that I can come back refreshed, stronger and better. I also need to be willing to take another's place to relieve them, but it also gives me the opportunity to learn and prepare to take my own place.

I have learnt the difference between personal responsibility and the shared responsibility that comes from interdependence on others. I have accepted that sometimes I will need a teammate to achieve the aim of my game.

JOGA BONITA 5

"Be not afraid of life. Believe that life is worth living, and your belief will help create the fact." – **William James**

THE SCORES: Points awarded for scoring goals. Usually displayed on a scoreboard for all to see.

The score is a measure to show you how well you are performing in the game. The only scores that matter are the ones that determine the outcome of your game. Just like in football, no matter how much possession your team had, no matter how many shots at goal, no matter how many corner kicks, the only thing that will matter when the final whistle is blown is how many goals were achieved.

It's not enough to have an aim, it's not enough to play by the rules, it's not even enough to have the right tools and techniques. All these things must work together to achieve a goal that counts – a goal that gives you mastery over your life's opponent. The score is an indication that you are fulfilling the aim of the game. Pay attention to the scores. You need to make the scores; you need to get your wins! It might take a while, frustration may set in but as long as you keep going diligently your break will surely come. You have to master those emotions, raise that child, build that career, write that business plan, be an encouragement, help someone in need, forgive and give that person another chance, love, be a true friend and the list could go on in the areas where you need to get your victories.

I have learnt that as much as life can be enjoyed, I must never forget my purpose and the goals that I need to achieve to get me on the scoreboard of the game.

THE FANS: These are the people in the stands watching the game, cheering on their team and jeering their opponents.

Most of your life will be lived before the eyes of another. There are those who will believe in you and your ability, who will stick with you and be on your side whether you fail or succeed. Some will be inspired by you, others will give up because of you. There is no escape from the spectre that your life is.

It is great to have fans, but at some point every good player will have to shut out the noise from the stands and focus on playing their game. It is quite daunting to think that you are always under scrutiny, that you always have to put your best foot forward. This can be a huge distraction from your aim in the game. I like this quote by Henry D. Thoreau, "Be yourself – not your idea of what you think somebody else's idea of yourself should be."

I have learnt that I should not let the fans define me, but rather let them celebrate me for the best me I can be. If I focus on putting my best foot forward then my weaker foot would be supporting the rest

of my body weight. Rather than putting my best foot forward, if I had two 'best feet' I would never have to worry about how I walked or stood and who saw me doing it.

THE OPPONENTS: I don't have much to say about the opponents, but there wouldn't be much of a game without them. The writer Thomas Merton says, "Souls are like athletes, that need opponents worthy of them, if they are to be tried and extended and pushed to the full use of their powers, and rewarded according to their capacity."

You can easily judge the strength or skill of a person by the type of opponent they are able to contend with and invariably overcome. I have learnt to appreciate the opponent for what they bring. They are a great opportunity for me to bring out my best game.

In conclusion, life can be lived beautifully, expressed to the maximum, enjoyed to the fullest, yielding the most awesome results when you learn how to play it right. In case you have been on a losing streak, you are probably on an ill-prepared side. It's not too late to change sides and hook-up with the champions in life. You are not too far down to reach out and begin to learn what it means to live life successfully.

Life is like a game. To me this statement does not trivialize the meaning of life, but it has simplified my understanding of it and what I need to do to ensure that I win at this game.

DISCRIMINATION

"People fail to get along because they fear each other; they fear each other because they don't know each other; they don't know each other because they have not communicated with each other." – **Martin Luther King Jr.**

I was born to an African father and a Caribbean mother and grew up in Nigeria. As I got older I began to experience the effects that describe a word I hardly knew existed, "Discrimination".

To discriminate is to make a distinction in favour of or against a person or thing on the basis of the group, class, or category to which the person or thing belongs rather than according to actual merit.

I was what they called 'Oyinbo' because my mother was supposedly one too. This meant I stood out in a category or class that my observers had determined. I usually got jeered at on the playgrounds, excluded by peers from participating in certain games, and picked on or bullied also. I did not fit in on account of my slightly fairer colour; a slight difference in my accent and the difference in my upbringing. It particularly did not help that I could not speak the language of my locality. All I wanted to be was accepted for who I was and fit in with the others.

I tried to cope with it in the following ways; playing down my traits that seemed to offend my persecutors; pretending to be someone I wasn't so that I could fit in a little better, dreaming that one day they would all realise what a wonderful person I was and accept me; finally, fighting back.

Fighting back became my favourite coping mechanism as the other options left me feeling more frustrated and very angry. I remember one day in secondary school when I took on one of my incessant bullies, I don't know where the strength came from but I gave him much more than he bargained for. Suffice it to say, he never bothered me again. In fact, we ended up being good friends.

I have since found that discrimination is rife all over the world and in all walks of life. Having moved over to the Western world where people are 'more educated' and 'open minded' did not reduce the percentage of my exposure to the discrimination index. In fact, it highlighted it to me but in a slightly different way. It is true that one can be discriminated against because of age, sex, race, social status, intellectual ability, disability, religion, personal convictions, unfounded perceptions or any other thing no matter how insignificant it may seem.

Being the recipient of discrimination is never easy and as much as we wish that it would go away, it abounds in every sphere of society. Sometimes the one that discriminates against you is only ignorant of who you are or maybe even fearful of you.

I have learned to evaluate myself in the face of discrimination assessing my qualities that seem to be offensive to another. In some cases, I need to represent myself better, in others I need to affirm that there is absolutely nothing wrong with me and then I fight back. Only this time I would not do so with physical punches, but with education and reassurance to the one that is ignorant and fearful.

I have learnt to accept myself for who I am and I make no apologies for it. I am not what I do or what I am perceived to be. My difference is not a disadvantage; my diversity is not a disaster. You may not want to be like me because what I am does not fit in with your personal preferences, but as I be the best that me is, you will come to acknowledge that being me must just be fantastic!

I am unique, I am intelligent, I am capable, I am strong, I am able, I am African, I am Caribbean, I am British too, I am a child of God, I am successful, I am progressive, I am kind, I am graceful, I am forgiving, I am human, I am alive, I am thankful, I am aware of who I am. I am blessed to be me.

Oyinbo is the Nigerian Yoruba language for white man. It is also commonly used to describe a foreigner.

SOMEBODY'S GOING TO DO IT – WHY NOT YOU?

"What would life be if we had no courage to attempt anything?"
– Vincent Van Gogh

I was on vacation in Jamaica in 2006 when I came across a billboard advertising Guinness. It had the caption "SOMEBODY'S GOING TO DO IT – WHY NOT YOU!" This got me thinking about a mind-set I had developed over the years.

While growing up, my parents – especially my Mum, would tell us what to do and what not to do. "Don't go out after 5pm.", "don't talk to strangers", "don't run across the road", "don't eat any more chocolates", "go and do your homework", "Go and take a bath", "Go to bed now!"

When we asked why we had all these restrictions and couldn't do the things we wanted, the reply was, "I want you to be good children and I don't want anything bad to happen to you." Their concerns were based on some unfortunate happenings to children that we knew or heard about. Things like, a child being hit by a car, somebody's child was kidnapped, another child got expelled from school and somebody's child was caught stealing. My parents didn't want that to be my siblings or me. I soon got the message that something was going to happen to somebody somewhere, and when it did, I was just glad that it wasn't me.

In my university years, there was anticipation of news from the rumour mills that kept the campus buzzing. It was clear that every semester somebody was going to get drunk, somebody was going to get pregnant, somebody was going to fail, somebody was going to drop out, somebody was going to get branded a troublemaker, somebody was going to get arrested. Somebody was going to do it or be it!

I realised that my association of somebody doing something that was worth talking about was always kind of negative. But as there were those landing in trouble, there was also somebody getting a distinction, somebody winning a scholarship, somebody getting an internship, and somebody graduating.

Why did I notice more of the 'bad things' I wondered? Well, I learned that nothing just happens, someone or something has to make it happen. The so-called troublemakers were a breed that had a special something that the goody two shoes never seemed to exhibit. They had guts! They made things happen. I guess that's what made them more popular and not necessarily the things that they did. The bad boy would step out of the class with all swag announcing that he was going to smoke his joint just outside the window and no one could stop him. We would all look on in disbelief and almost applaud him as he turned to leave. I never heard the smartest boy in class announce with

such boldness, conviction and authority that he was going to smash sorry pass his tests. Maybe that's why I never took too much notice of who did the 'good' things.

The one with guts is not afraid to try, or fail at trying. The one with guts pushes the boundaries of the norm and seeks to accomplish what has never been done. The one with guts honestly believes that they can do it no matter what the task. To the one with guts, impossible is nothing. They don't care if the world around them says it can't be done, they are determined to prove everyone else wrong.

The decision to do something noble is commendable, but it's the guts to do it that distinguishes the good (intentions) from the great (achievements). As the saying goes, "no guts, no glory".

I have learnt to have guts and be the one to do the next great thing. Somebody's going to birth the next great idea, somebody's going to eradicate a disease, somebody's going to educate a continent, somebody's going to raise a president, somebody's going to start a multibillion pound business, somebody's going to stop a conflict, somebody's going to inspire a generation, somebody's message is going to reach a billion people, somebody's life is going to make a remarkable difference. Why not me? Why not me!

THE PHILOSOPHY OF (A) FAILURE

"Negative results are just what I want. They're just as valuable to me as positive results. I can never find the thing that does the job best until I find the ones that don't." – **Thomas A. Edison**

No one wants to be classified as a failure as most of our societies place a stigma on the unfortunate soul that has been labelled as one. The topic of failure is not the idea of a conversation that most people care to have; in contrast, they would rather explore their more sterling achievements.

As a child at primary school in Nigeria, I noticed that failure was frowned upon. Pupils were punished for not knowing the right answer. I hated art classes because the art teacher was always poised and ready to dish out his punishment to the one who failed to sketch the bowl of fruit 'right'.

Parents were not that supportive either, and I knew of some children who would cry profusely and dread going home because of an 'F' on their report cards. The view we developed on failure was that it must not happen, and when it did one felt so low, dejected and condemned.

A strong impression was created in my mind that teachers and parents were immune to this thing called failure and I just couldn't wait to grow up to attain this invincible status.

I developed a fear of failure for the obvious reasons like most other people. If failing is to fall short of an attempted, expected or desired achievement, then, to be afraid of failure is to be afraid to try again. This fear makes expectations and desires of achievement burdensome.

I soon found that the typical traits one would display to cope with the appearance of anything that looked like failure were excuses, denials and cover-ups. This was quite typical of the 'grown-ups'. Another key one was to philosophise.

I love this quote attributed to the Greek philosopher Socrates, *"By all means, marry. If you get a good wife, you'll become happy; if you get a bad one, you'll become a philosopher."*

Have you ever noticed that failure somehow brings about the philosopher in you? To philosophise is to investigate the truths and principles of knowledge and in its original form in the Greek language it connotes the love of knowledge.

Every failure knowingly or unknowingly is seeking to understand why they failed and then they draw some knowledge from that experience. This let me know that a failure is no fool. For if my failure gets me to reflect on my actions and draw out a philosophy from it, then I have gained something valuable, as opposed to the fool who is unequivocally uninterested in any form of wisdom.

One day I challenged my fear of failure because I thought to myself, "I am mostly afraid of the difficult things that I think I cannot do or have not done, like jumping out of a plane in a sky dive, starting a business, or getting married. But to fail is so easy, common and perhaps inevitable, so why should it fall into the category of things I fear?

Training to become a professional like a Consultant could take years, however, to fail at little things along the way gives me a quick lesson with a quick qualification, making me a quick professional in that little area. Embracing the quick lessons over the years has led me to become that seasoned professional. I have never seen a professor who is afraid of his area of expertise, so why should I be afraid of what I have unwantedly become an expert at (failure)?" These thoughts ended my fear of failure.

Failure is not a bad thing in itself if it leads you to discover a philosophy – a love for knowledge – that makes you a better person than you were before you failed. It is however the fear of failure that will seek to paralyse you from ever trying again. And once you fail to try again you remain where you are, in the place of failure.

In his attempts to invent a light bulb, Thomas Edison was known to have said, "I have not failed. I've just found 5,000 ways that won't work". His philosophy of failure made him thrive as one of the greatest inventors of modern time.

I have learnt to develop a philosophy from my failings, which prompts me not to hide but rather share my experiences of failure with someone who might be gripped by the fear of failure. When one is free from the fear of failure, then one is truly free to succeed.

KEEP LEARNING

"The more I live, the more I learn. The more I learn, the more I realize, the less I know." – **Michel Legrand**

A few decades back the average Nigerian parent drummed it into the ears of their children that they needed an education to have a better life. As a people we became very keen on getting the qualifications associated with it. We spent at least 16 to 20 of our early years in one school system or the other trying to gain the noble status of being called educated. When I cast my mind back to all the friends and acquaintances I made during those years, I see a very small percentage who actually make a living from their 'educational' qualifications. We erroneously believed that going through that system made us learned and that after gaining the highest degree we were ready to take on the world. I have since changed my mind about seeing education as an end in itself rather than a means to an end.

Education according to the dictionary is – the act or process of imparting or acquiring knowledge or skills. The original word originates from Latin – EDUCERE and is broken down as follows; EX – "out" and DUCERE – "to lead". Putting them together, it means to lead out, or to bring out. Education then by its very meaning is to bring out what is already in you in a measure. An apprenticeship most closely mirrors the essence of the original word used to describe education. The apprentice completes their formal or informal training with the acquisition of knowledge, skill and most importantly the ability to replicate the business that their mentor has taught.

We need to ask, have we left our formal education with an encouragement in the thing that we are gifted to do? Did it teach us to deal with life outside the walls of the institution? Did it equip us to go out there and take action capable of producing tangible results? Are we any more enlightened than when we started that journey? Are we any closer to being a valuable addition to our society?

Some of the most successful people on the planet today never completed a formal education like we know it. They don't have degrees or certificates of learning yet their knowledge and influence in their fields of endeavour cannot be denied. In spite of their lack of formal education, one thing is clear with this group; they have never stopped learning. In fact, it seems they understand and appreciate the value of learning more than those who went through a formal system. Someone said, "If you get one degree, remember that there are 360 of them in a circle." These folk understand this well and never assume to have acquired the golden key of knowledge, rather they seek to add to what they already know. This brings me to an important point; the best education anyone can receive is one where the student is taught to learn and encouraged to keep learning. Malcolm Forbes said, "Education's purpose is to replace an empty mind with an open one."

When I was about 10, my father was building a house for the family on a land he had acquired, and each time we visited the site, I would watch the workmen as they mixed the cement, laid the bricks, cut the wood, bent the iron bars, painted the walls, and fixed the tiles. I would always ask questions and sometimes they would let me try my hand at some of their tasks. This was so exciting for me and I learnt a great deal about construction from them. Most of the men who taught me these skills had minimal formal education..

Years later when I moved to the United Kingdom to study, I started job hunting after completing my course but was unable to secure a professional role for quite a while. My funds were terribly low and there was a period where for weeks I could not afford to buy any food after scraping together what little I had to pay my rent. I became desperate and had to pick up a job as a care worker and also as a security guard. I needed a large amount of money to pay off some of my school bills and my earnings couldn't get me there. One day a friend asked me if I knew anyone who could do a good paint job, I thought to myself, "Why is she asking me?" I was about to say no when I had a flash back on the things I had learnt at my father's building site. I said "yes, I could". After a bit of persuasion and recounting the stories from my past, I was given the job. Over the next few weeks' word got out about the quality of my work and I soon acquired more work for painting, flooring, tiling etc. Within a couple of months I had a healthy sum of money to pay off my debts.

It is a great opportunity to have been blessed with the privilege of a formal education, but it is an even greater one to be equipped with everything I need to keep on learning. So, no matter who the teacher appears to be and where the lesson tends to take place, I keep learning for there will be someone who knows something better than I do and their tutorial could benefit me greatly. I have learnt to be a student of life because therein lies my growth as a person. I now frequently ask the question, "What can I do with what I just learnt?"

THE ANT

"All good work is done the way ants do things: little by little"
– Lafcadio Hearn

No one seems to like being called small. Where I grew up, it was the height of an insult to be called an ant.

When two people came to a stand-off – Adults, children, male or female alike – you would hear one say "who do you think you are? Look at this small ant talking to me!" Of course the other would feel most insulted and then the fracas would ensue.

Size can be relative depending on the thing in question, but whatever it is; there is always the big, average and small of it. Most would immediately opt for the big or at least average; no one wants the small.

Most ladies want Mr Tall, dark and handsome, never Dr Short, stout and jolly.

We want a big pay check, a big house, a big TV, a big business, a big discount, a big favour, a big portion, a big idea, a big opportunity and some big other-things that are not appropriate to write about.

If one is not careful, it is so easy to despise the small things and almost forget that most things that became big started from something very small.

The ant is a very small creature, yet there are so many lessons we can learn from it. It is known for industry – they plan, prepare, save, build, and work hard. It is known for community – with roles and responsibilities that each follows for the greater good of the colony. It is known for survivability – ants are found everywhere and scientists believe that 15-25% of all animal biomass is made up of ants.

The ant goes through 4 stages of development. The egg – at this point other ants carry them – this shows dependence. The Larvae – other ants feed them – showing dependence. The Pupae – other ants leave them alone to develop in its own space – showing independence. The Imago – the fully formed adult comes out and takes on roles and responsibilities within the colony, giving back the same care that it received in its early life – showing interdependence. Ants have two stomachs, one to hold food for itself and the other to hold food for its fellows.

One can observe from the ant certain traits that help it to maintain such a laudable reputation:

The ant is Constant – You have to be consistent, doing what is right, when you feel like and when you don't, in season and out of season.

Compliant – you must line up with the required standards of life. Your internal capabilities must be developed to meet your external demands.

Accountant – give a good report of yourself and your actions.

Vigilant – be aware of what is in your surroundings and how you can use it to your advantage.

When you imbibe some of the attitudes of the ant, you can move from being dormant to becoming valiant. The once detestable immigrant can become a sought out celebrant. The insignificant can become the commandant.

It doesn't matter that they call you an ant, as long as you can be brilliant, exuberant, fragrant, gallant, tolerant, pleasant, adamant, aspirant, vibrant, and jubilant. Then they will have no choice but to acknowledge that you are important.

I have learnt that size doesn't matter as long as I have inculcated the right attitude and am doing the right things even at a small size; working not just for myself but for the greater good of my fellow man. An ant that is too relevant to the world around it, acting with an attitude that is brilliant will be given the honour that is reserved for the Giant.

You can watch a short video clip produced for this writing on YouTube, search "The Ant by Olaolu Opebiyi".

HOLDER FOLDER

"Observation more than books and experience more than persons, are the prime educators." – **Amos Bronson Alcott**

I remember the song by the country western singer, Kenny Rogers, called 'The Gambler'. The lyrics of the refrain go something like this:

You've got to know when to hold 'em

Know when to fold 'em

Know when to walk away

Know when to run

You never count your money

When you're sittin' at the table

There'll be time enough for countin'

When the dealin's done

The gambler seemed to be an expert at his card game for he knew what to hold on to and let go of at the right moment in time. There is a truth in what the gambler had to say, as it is wise to hold on to what is an advantage, and fold – let go of - what could cause damage.

Have you ever used expressions like: "He can't hold down a good job"? "She didn't hold on to her man". "He tried to hold a meaningful conversation with her". "He failed to hold up his end of the bargain". "She knows how to hold her own". "Get a hold of yourself!" "Hold your tongue". "Hold your head up high". "I hold him in high esteem".

Well, one key attribute of effective people is their ability to hold on to things. To hold something for long enough is to keep it in a stable condition. Stability is a good ground for growth and success. You sometimes need to hold on to certain disciplines or habits for long enough until they become a part of you.

I have learnt of 6 main areas where there is a need to develop the ability to hold or fold things in order to release my greatest potential.

1. Hold Observation

The human mind has been designed in such a way that allows it to absorb knowledge quickest by means of observation. Personal development researchers say that we learn 83% through sight, 11% through hearing, 3.5% through smell, 1.5% through touch and 1% through taste.

Observation gives birth to thinking and learning. If one can hold observation for long enough, thoughts that produce dividends of applicable knowledge will surely crystalize.

From the stats above, it appears that experience is not necessarily the best teacher as only 6% of what is learnt about the world around us is by experience (touch, taste and smell).

Environment is very important to observation. If you are in a positive environment, you will observe positive things and therefore think positively. The same is true if you happen to be in the wrong environment, your thinking will eventually be all wrong. The outcome of observation then is almost synonymous with the environment in which it happens.

I keep reminding myself that my greatest learning comes from my ability to hold my observations. I also assess the kind of environment I am exposed to as this influences what I eventually learn. I can change my environment – if not physically, then through the stories of others spoken in conversation, written in books or recorded in multimedia. This makes me discipline myself to change my environment from time to time by the various means mentioned to ensure that I am putting things into proper perspective as the world is much bigger than my personal view of it.

HOLDER FOLDER 2

"Accuracy of observation is the equivalent of accuracy of thinking."
– Wallace Stevens

I have talked about the ability to hold on to observation, which is the most effective way that the human mind picks up knowledge.

As a student of science I totally enjoyed those classes where we carried out experiments. I remember once in a chemistry lab, my classmate and I decided to abandon the experimental guide and mix our own reagents for fun. We mixed up a solution that began to bubble in the test tube and before you could say Jack Robinson, the test tube exploded releasing a gas that made us feel like we were going to pass out. We quickly abandoned the lab.

Science teaches us to observe the world around us, but such observations must be recorded and then interpreted. That information is then filed away for imminent or future actions.

So how do we process our observations and what do we do with them?

This brings me to another important thing to hold on to – Contemplation.

2. Hold Contemplation (Thinking)

We live in a world that is driven by triggers. According to the laws of motion, an object that is stationary remains so until it is disturbed to attain motion. Actions are followed by reactions, just like calls are followed by responses. Nothing just happens, even in the realm of our thoughts. Thoughts need triggers. I never get offended by people I did not notice, but as soon as I notice that they did not respond when I said hello, or they looked at me funny (trigger), I begin to think, "that person doesn't seem to like me". I would never have thought it if I never observed it.

Constructive positive thinking is hard work because once thinking has been triggered it must be sustained. I like this quote that says, "The mind is not a vessel to be filled, but a fire to be kindled."

The problem with fire is that it goes out if it is not supplied with enough fuel to keep burning.

What we observe is like a matchstick that kindles a light in our mind but only for a few moments. I have learnt to take that transient spark and hold it on the candle of my contemplation until I am able to extract and distil wisdom for action from what I have observed.

Information and ideas bombard me every day and I need to retain some of them if I am to be more effective with my life.

There are two things I have learnt to practice to strengthen the hold on my contemplation. They are meditation and documentation. To meditate is to reflect on a thought, i.e. to revisit that thought; just like a cow regurgitates the grass it had eaten earlier to chew it properly for digestion in the stomach. Documentation – I write down my thoughts about an issue so I don't forget what I observed and thought initially.

Hold on to observation and contemplation.

HOLDER FOLDER 3

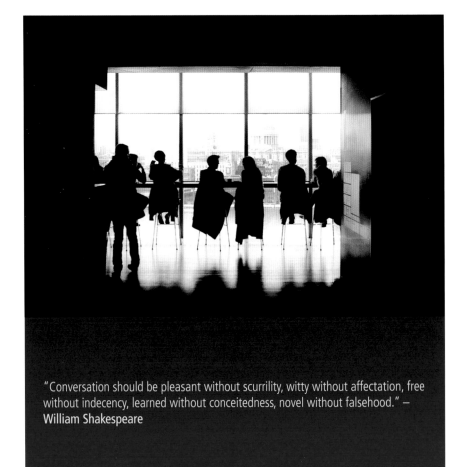

"Conversation should be pleasant without scurrility, witty without affectation, free without indecency, learned without conceitedness, novel without falsehood." – William Shakespeare

Until you are able to clearly communicate what you are thinking, you virtually remain a stranger to the world around you. You never truly get to know the personality of another person until they speak.

Have you ever been captivated at the sight of that tall dark and handsome guy or the lady who stood out like a rose in the midst of thorn bushes? Then you heard them speak…!

Whatever your observation and the contemplation of it, you must be able to share it in conversation. The third thing I learnt to hold is a conversation.

3. Hold Conversation (Speech)

Conversations are powerful tools that are used to convince, convict, command, influence, reveal, express, etc. They can make or break. Every important aspect of our lives will be decided as a result of a conversation.

A proposal for a relationship is a conversation. Buying and selling is done through conversation. An interview is a conversation. Carrying out our daily work tasks is punctuated by conversation. Deals are sealed in a conversation. Prayer is a conversation.

Conversations are too important for one to mess about with. You have to hold a conversation until you are able to get to your desired aim. An older friend of mine who gets quite comical in sharing his unique perspectives on things once pointed out to me someone he reckoned had "diarrhoea of the mouth and constipation of ideas".

No one wants to be in the company of one such person that babbles on aimlessly for hours, but on the other extreme though, it is tough trying to speak to someone who won't give much of a response in a conversation.

Conversation must be held at the appropriate level with the appropriate people. It is one of the great arts most people assume that an individual possesses naturally or that one lacks instinctively, however, the ability to do it right can be learned and practised until the student becomes a master at it.

I have learnt the importance and power of being able to hold the right conversation, but also to fold up the wrong ones. The tongue is a powerful thing and the one that uses it right in conversation will be formidable in their endeavours.

You may be one conversation away from your biggest breakthrough. Learn how to communicate properly and speak out your refined contemplation. Who knows what the next conversation you hold will bring.

Hold on to observation, contemplation and conversation.

HOLDER FOLDER 4

"Dear George: Remember no man is a failure who has friends."
– It's a wonderful life (a film)

There are two categories of people that we tend to be wary of; those who always want to give us a piece of their mind and those who seldom speak their mind. We avoid the former because they usually air their less than beautiful opinions and end up soiling our atmosphere or mood, and we are suspicious of the latter because we never really know what they are thinking. It is a difficult task to maintain a relationship with such people.

On the other hand, there are those who have a much more balanced expression of their thoughts, packaged in words that endear us to them. It is important to be this kind of person – the one whose contemplation and conversation brings them into positive relationship with others. The fourth thing I have learnt to hold on to is relation.

4. Hold Relations

A good conversation is an open door that leads one into the possibility of a new relationship.

This applies to all, from the prime leader of a nation, establishment or movement, to the young child making a new friend at school. What is said has the potential to win hearts and minds.

People are important, and most times they hold the key to new experiences that we want to enter. They become a kind of gatekeeper to those things.

When I was growing up, no one needed to tell me that mummy was the gatekeeper to good things like sweets and ice cream. As long as I was a 'good boy' and did those things she approved of, I got my regular fix. When I failed to hold up my end of this mutually beneficial relationship, I missed out on my goodies.

Do you remember the gatekeepers to the cliques you so wanted to be a part of in high school? As long as they were your friends, everyone in the group was fine with you, but when you fell out with them, the whole group turned its back on you. I fell out with such a gatekeeper once in primary school, and when everyone turned their back on me, I took matters into my own hands by roughing him up pretty badly. I eventually made that relationship good by revisiting the basics for establishing one – good conversation.

Holding on to the right relationship is an important factor that can make or break us. There is a proverb that says "show me your friends and I will tell you who you are."

Who do you want to be? There is someone, somewhere who is key to helping you be that person. You need to find them and initiate a relationship with them, holding on to it until that connection serves it purpose. You may not always like their personality when you first notice them, and maybe that has even put you off from trying to get close. But until you really take out time to speak with them you might not correct your initial impressions, which could have been wrong. There is a mentor, leader, coach, comrade, confidant, helper, adviser, friend, that is your next relationship to success, but you are the one to initiate it.

How many have been overlooked for a promotion, lost out on a business deal, discounted for the admission, rejected at the interview and such like? This is not necessarily because they did not work hard enough to deserve it, but they did not take the time to initiate or hold on to certain relationships that would have kept them in view of the gatekeeper. I have learnt that no matter how skilled I may be I still need to develop relationships that would promote my skills to the gatekeepers because people would rather deal with one that they know and trust.

Hold on to observation, contemplation, conversation and relation.

HOLDER FOLDER 5

"Do you want to know who you are? Don't ask. Act! Action will delineate and define you." – **Thomas Jefferson**

Integrity is one of the most sterling virtues that one can possess. It is our thoughts aligning with our words; our actions in harmony with our principles. Our conduct will speak for us more eloquently than our words ever could.

Saying what I will do and doing what I have said will form the basic foundation of trust in any relationship with another. This is the ground on which reputation is built until it becomes a standard that can be relied upon.

The fifth thing I have learnt to hold is action!

5. Hold Action

Who do you want to be? What are you trying to achieve? Where are you attempting to get to? Who would you love to be with? What must you have? You can't desire to be the world's marathon champion and only run half a mile every other day after lunch. Your action right there just informed me of your priority.

It is by action that one proves their interest in a thing. Do you want to hold on to that relationship, job, physique, promotion, property, access, or membership? Then, there is something that you must start or continue to do to maintain or attain it. Once you set the priority by your consistent actions, chances are you will succeed.

It is consistent action in any field that guarantees sure results. The only instance in which a first time participant could be a winner is in the lottery (and such likes), and the chances of winning are 1 in possibly 100 million (depending on how many others are participating).

Your action in your chosen endeavour however can make you a master at it and even though there are about 6 billion people on the planet, you are guaranteed a better outcome from action than if you played the lottery.

At reproduction, you were one sperm cell among possibly 40-500 million all aiming to fertilize a single ovum. However, your action of swimming towards the goal without giving up set you apart from so many others, and here you are today.

Know this, your action reduces the odds of the number of people that are able to compete against you in any area you have chosen to focus. After a while, it refines you remarkably bringing out your very best until the only competition left will be with yourself. This is where you become the one to reference in your area of enterprise and beyond.

As you develop, you start out taking actions that are general to everyone, but there comes a time when through experience you develop a set of actions unique only to you and performed by you. This is what sets you apart from the best of us even though you are as common as the rest of us. Everyone sings, but the actions you have taken with your voice make you stand out. Many are married, but your actions have made your home heaven on earth. There are multitudes of speakers, but your actions have made you an orator par excellence.

I want to cultivate my set of actions that distinguish me from the rest and make me the best I was born to be. I want to hold on to actions that refine me, define me and confine me to greatness!

Hold on to observation, contemplation, conversation, relation and action.

HOLDER FOLDER 6

"The art of war teaches us to rely not on the likelihood of the enemy's not coming, but on our own readiness to receive him; not on the chance of his not attacking, but rather on the fact that we have made our position unassailable." – **Sun Tzu**

Consistent action will give you a name and establish you as a brand that can be trusted. This status needs to be preserved and protected. It is said that Rome was not built in a day, however there are historians who believe that the city was destroyed in a single night.

It does not matter how long it has taken you to achieve something great, the transience of the world we live in makes it possible to lose it all in one unguarded moment. Do not despair because there is something that can be done to guard against that happening.

The sixth thing I have learnt to hold is my position.

6. Hold Position

There are many quotes about the wisdom of starting all over when things have gone badly wrong. It takes strength, courage and character to go back to the drawing board. Sometimes, what is recreated is a lot better than what initially existed.

Even though this may be true, it is likely that one may have gone through several cycles of a restart and come out with a pretty good position in life. At this point the lesson of starting over is well known, so rather than go through that cycle again, one must develop a strong commitment to protecting the growth and achievements attained.

Remember the proverbial thief that came in the night? If the householder knew when he would come, he would have prepared himself against an invasion. So, instead of anticipating when the thief will come, why not just live prepared, live ready.

In business circles, there is a lot of talk about risk and how to mitigate it. Companies ask, "what do we do to hold our position of service if things go wrong?" These are the types of establishments that you hear are holding their market share – they are holding their position in the market place.

Your life is worth more than any business venture, so what are the risks that you may be exposed to which could bring you down, and how do you mitigate them? Answering these questions helps you to maintain and protect the position you have attained and reduce the possibility of losing it overnight.

There is a lesson to be learnt from the tree. It stands in its position, holding on to the ground with its roots and passing through all kinds of adverse weather. Even though it looks like it is going nowhere fast, that tree knows it has found good ground and is growing somewhere slowly but surely. The plant that creeps everywhere is nowhere to be found after 100 years, while the tree becomes the landmark in that same place.

If you have found the thing that is good for your life's growth, you need to hold on to it and grow. There is no need to change your position; there is no need to shift ground. Stand your ground, maintain your position and sustain your growth.

I don't want to slip back into what I used to be or where I started from, which was average and common. I want to hold on to where I am now and use it as a springboard to reach where I should grow next.

Hold on to observation, contemplation, conversation, relation, action and position.

HOLDER FOLDER 7

"Anyone can give up, it's the easiest thing in the world to do. But to hold it together when everyone else would understand if you fell apart, that's true strength." – **Unknown**

I wish there was just one thing I needed to do to get all the results I desired in every part of my life. But the reality is that it takes a combination of steps or actions that are finely coordinated to actually achieve a result. For instance, did you know that 12 facial muscles are involved in the simple act of smiling? I bet you thought the only muscles for this action were your lips.

There are several things that we learn every day, and no one thing in itself produces what we desire but a combination of them do. In these modern times of quick fixes, fast results and the microwave, we are sometimes thrown into shock for a few moments when we encounter some process that still requires several steps and much waiting to make them work. But we must remember, every good thing that will stand the test of time takes a while to be put together.

That is why I have learnt one final thing – to hold it all together.

7. Hold it All Together

Holding it together is the key to making a system work for you. The bicycle handle is important, but so are the wheels, chain, brakes or pedals. If I tried to cycle with the handle only, I would be going nowhere even though I steered it in the direction I should be headed. It is all the parts held together that give me the momentum I desire to reach my destination.

I found I made good progress in any area of my life where I held together my observations, contemplations, conversations, relations, actions, and positions.

I have been in situations where my job was not making the progress I would like. Applying these principles, I would **observe** my environment looking out for what and who were considered good for the job. I then **contemplated** what I could do to be and contribute to the good. Next I went about engaging my colleagues and managers in **conversations** about what good looked like and the best way to achieve it. This usually led to more open **relations** with those that were like-minded. I then began to take **action** on those ideas I had shared or learned and before long my **position** within the team changed for the better. It has worked for my marriage, finances, business plans and all areas of my life.

Sometimes you don't want to look at it, or think about it or talk about it or be around it or do it or be it. Whenever you are tempted to feel that way remember this quote – "Anyone can give up, it's the easiest thing in the world to do. But to hold it together when everyone else would understand if you fell apart, that's true strength." – Unknown.

I have learnt to focus on the things I should hold onto, and improved my speed of folding up the things I should let go of.

Hold it all together – observation, contemplation, conversation, relation, action and position.

SOMETHING FOR TOMORROW

"Throw moderation to the winds, and the greatest pleasures bring the greatest pains." – Democritus

From my little experiences so far, I have noted that too much of any particular thing is bad for you, just as too little of it is detrimental. When does a thing become too much or too little? This question can only be answered in relation to how that thing is meant to be used. Too much salt can lead to high blood pressure and heart disease, whereas too little can lead to a condition known as Hyponatremia, which could result in seizures. In the same vein, believe it or not, too much water can kill you with over hydration and too little leads to dehydration. The amount of salt recommended per day is about 6 grams or one teaspoon full, while the amount of water recommended per day is a weight of 2kg (2 litres – 9 tea cups full).

In view of this, getting the right balance seems key in our ability to thrive. The more one masters how to get the balance right, the more they are able to benefit from their experiences. One of the secrets to good cooking is to get the right proportions of the ingredients into the meal.

Going down memory lane, I can still hear my mum chiding "leave something for tomorrow!" "Waste not, want not!" I only got one scoop of ice cream even though I wanted five, but I had to leave something for tomorrow. We were only allowed to watch one video film a day, so that we could have something left for tomorrow. I would have loved to stay in the pool for much longer than two hours, again, some things had to be done next time. It became a mantra that guided everything that we did. We were restrained from over indulging in the things we enjoyed, but at the same time made to participate in the things we did not care for like tidying up, homework, eating our greens, etc., so we could have something better for tomorrow.

When I left home to be on my own for the first time, I had all the time and resources I needed to do what I wanted. I was free! So, I tried to enjoy all I could for as long as I could. However, I soon discovered that my original estimation of how much time and resources I had was greatly skewed. Reality quickly set in at about the same time that hunger – uninvited – decided to squat with me. It had moved in when my senses had moved out to have a good time. When I came back to myself, like the prodigal son, the words of my mum suddenly made sense "waste not, want not", "leave something for tomorrow!" Her lesson on moderation hit home.

I used to think that moderation was about taking the fun out of things, but I have learnt that moderation doesn't mean playing down on the enthusiasm, focus or drive you have for a thing; rather it means giving the right amounts of focus and drive to those things. Moderation is about pacing yourself with what you have left in your tank to get to the desired goal, finishing strong.

There is always something that needs to be left for tomorrow so you can go on and focus on the rest of what is needful for today.

I WENT TO GHANA

"The best thinking has been done in solitude. The worst has been done in turmoil." – **Thomas A. Edison**

On the 14th of April 2008, I arrived at the Kotoka international airport in Accra, Ghana, where I lived for just over 2 months. The Republic of Ghana is a sovereign state located along the Gulf of Guinea and Atlantic Ocean, in the sub region of West Africa. Ghana is the 82nd largest country in the world and 33rd largest country on Continental Africa by landmass.

So why did I go to Ghana? I am not Ghanaian, even though my Nigerian father was born there in the late 1930's.

The six years preceding my trip to Ghana were extremely busy for me. I had completed a Master's degree at a university in London, and then the job search began. It was not smooth sailing in those days, as I had to work all sorts of jobs to make ends meet. I worked at a mental care home; then as a security officer, and as a handy man, pretty much at about the same time. I eventually got a regular job almost 2 years into doing all this.

It was great to be working at a level I was educated for, and the first few years in employment were greeted with a lot of enthusiasm and hard work. I put all my energy into what I was doing, but after a while fatigue began to set in for several reasons. The general vicissitudes of life have a way of chipping away at the mettle of a man, but also backed up by the awareness of expending so much effort and obtaining very little results. Not to mention the work place politics, the sometimes mindless routine of the job, failed expectations from others, tumultuous relationships, personal disappointments, and so on, one gets worn down pretty quickly.

I got to the place where I became tired, burnt out, uninspired and safely on the slippery slope downwards to deep depression. I just did not have anything left in me to give. At this point all I could think of was how much I wanted to get away from everything and everyone. I felt the lyrics of the song by Lenny Kravitz, "I want to get away, I want to fly away, yeah yeah …".

After some serious soul searching, I knew that for my own good I needed to take a break. As I talked about my desire to go away to a place where I would not have to worry about bills, was not known by friends or family, and would have some solitude; a close friend of mine mentioned that I could go to Ghana and stay with his Dad.

I was single at the time and living with other guys in a rented apartment, so without too many commitments I started working out how to make my great escape to Ghana. First, I thought about how much time I would need to take off work; then I requested sabbatical leave and this was graciously granted (without pay I might add). I moved all my stuff into storage for a 3-month period – I didn't have much so it cost me very little to do this. I worked out all running costs for that time and cancelled all non-essential subscriptions; direct debits etc., until there was nothing limiting me financially from making the trip. Oh yes the ticket to Ghana! Well another good friend of mine worked with an airline and so he got me a round-trip ticket to Ghana for less than £200.

I needed inspiration, motivation, encouragement, vision and a clear plan for what I wanted to do with the rest of my life. People had said great encouraging things to me, but there comes a time when only you can find the strength that you need deep down within yourself. I took with me loads of books and past diaries so I could study and reflect. I was going to rest, read, think, and pray.

Planning this trip gave me a new focus, desire and drive that I had not had for a while. I already began to feel positive just knowing I was finally getting away.

One of the most important lessons I have learnt is that sometimes you need to plan a well thought-through getaway and then actually follow that plan through. It creates a new season in your life.

I WENT TO GHANA 2

"By three methods we may learn wisdom: First, by reflection, which is noblest; Second, by imitation, which is easiest; and third by experience, which is the bitterest." – Confucius

Real thinking is hard work. A lot of times we are on autopilot and not really thinking about the next steps for the future. Thinking is a discipline that should be developed. There is a difference between thoughts that pass through your mind toll-free, and thoughts that are held, processed and then made to yield dividends for you. I was reminded of the difference between the two in Ghana.

After about a week of sightseeing and resting, I began to read books, autobiographies, motivational writings and then my diaries - I must have taken about 30 different titles. This created an atmosphere around me with an outlook filled with great expectations for my future. A week or so later, I actually began to hear my thoughts, they were clear, unbiased, balanced and like a breath of fresh air. It was like renewing acquaintances with myself once again.

You never realize how cluttered and bogged down your mind becomes when you are being bombarded with one thousand and one things from the hustle and bustle of day-to-day living. It takes much effort to maintain the sanity of one's perspective under those circumstances.

For the next few weeks I capitalized on my newfound power of clear thinking to develop plans for my future and also strategies to ensure I would not allow myself to end up being so bogged down that I could not function. I analysed my past experiences and drew lessons from mistakes I had made. I reminded myself of the values that I had learned over the years; I noted my areas of strength and weaknesses. I thought about where I would want to be in the years following and I drew wisdom from the things I had read. I didn't just do a mental exercise; I wrote all of this down in detail so I would always remember what I had identified as being important to me.

When I eventually returned from Ghana to continue the 'rat race', I was refreshed, energized and different. Yes, the business of life still took its toll, but this time I was in a better place to keep it from wearing me down. From time to time I would go back to the notes that I had written and remind myself of my escape to Ghana.

Now that I am married with children, I don't know how possible it would be to embark on such a life altering adventure for that length of time, but one thing I do know is that I will not wait until I need it before making the adjustments that would keep me strong enough to continue to progress with my life.

The lessons I learnt from this experience were simple enough:

1. Take out time to rest, recover and reflect when things are getting too daunting

2. Planning to get away even if only for a few days is great therapy already helping you to escape from unbelievably pressured circumstances

3. Find a way to disconnect from all your day to-day responsibilities for that period. Remember if you fell down dead, your replacement would possibly be found before your burial

4. Your phone and other communication devices are only for emergency contact. Switch them off!

5. Take a few good books and read

6. It might take a few days and you may have to wrestle with your mind, but let it come to a place of uncluttered thinking

7. Pray or meditate if you know how to

8. Write down the things that come out of your time away

These things can actually be practiced on a small scale daily, weekly or monthly to keep you refreshed. The more you practice, the easier it becomes.

I am glad I went to Ghana, and for the things I experienced there.

WHAT DOES IT TAKE TO BE A PIONEER?

"Revolutions are brought about by men, by men who think as men of action and act as men of thought." – **Kwame Nkrumah**

When I was in Ghana, I noticed a strong sense of patriotism and pride among the people that was quite infectious. I was advised over and over again that I must see the museum that housed the tomb of Late Dr. Kwame Nkrumah.

He was a great African thought leader who among others led the movement for independence of African states from colonial rule. Ghana became the first independent African nation with Dr. Nkrumah being its first prime minister in 1957 and then president in 1960. He was also responsible for spearheading the formation of the Organisation of African Unity (OAU).

Born in September 1909, into very lowly circumstances in a village called Nkroful, he studied to be a teacher and taught at a girl's school for 5 years. In 1935, on his way to the United States for further studies, he passed through Liverpool in the United Kingdom and there he heard of the Invasion of Abyssinia (Ethiopia) by the Italian army. This event outraged him and sparked off his interest in the arena of politics. Nkrumah encountered political thought leaders with leanings towards Marxist ideologies during his sojourn in the United States and they taught him a thing or two about how underground movements worked. In 1945, he then returned to the United Kingdom with several degrees in Law, Education, Theology and Philosophy. It was there that he founded the West African National Secretariat to work towards the decolonization of Africa.

After returning to Ghana in 1947, he was active in the political scene and later formed the Convention People's Party. Through a decade of several challenges including arrests, detention in jails, learning to govern, unifying the four territories of Ghana and trying to win independence from the United Kingdom, Dr. Nkrumah emerged triumphant as he declared on the 6th of March 1957 that Ghana was an independent nation.

In the year 2000, 28 years after his death, he was voted Africa's man of the millennium by listeners of the BBC World Service. He was described by the BBC as a "Hero of Independence," and an "International symbol of freedom as the leader of the first black African country to shake off the chains of colonial rule." At the 100th anniversary of Kwame Nkrumah's birth, 21st September was declared to be Founder's Day, a statutory holiday in Ghana to celebrate the legacy of the Patriarch.

I was deeply inspired by the accounts of his life and it made me wonder, "what made this man such an iconic leader in and beyond his times?"

I learnt some inspiring lessons from the life and legacy of Dr. Kwame Nkrumah as listed below:

1. He had a desire to learn and educate himself

2. He had a heart for people

3. He found a purpose that he was willing to fight for and even die for

4. He had a discipline to apply what he had learnt and encouraged others to do the same

5. He had great vision

6. He never set out to have a career as a pioneer; he just focused on solving the problems that he saw

7. He was passionate about empowering others

He had his dark moments and misjudgements – like we all do; and even though later on in his political career he was exiled from his beloved Ghana, he continued to maintain a vision and desire to see the African continent free.

I can think of other African and indeed world leaders who were pioneers in their own right, most of whom did not set out to be, yet I could see working in their lives very similar principles to that of Dr. Nkrumah.

Will I be the next pioneer? I may not be able to answer that question, but I am hoping that the purpose I pursue and the problems I solve will.

RESPONSIBILITY

"The price of greatness is responsibility." – Winston Churchill

Responsibility! I have come to know this word to be synonymous with work. I was always encouraged as a child to be more responsible, in other words, cut out too much fun and games, be more serious. One was considered responsible when they cleaned the floor, did their homework, cooked the food, fetched the water, washed the dishes, ironed the clothes etc. The responsible adult has even more work to do. He/she takes care of those around them, drives the car, pays the bills, takes out the bin, fixes the broken light bulbs, runs a business, works a 9 to 5 job, and so on. The result being that at the end of a day Mr. /Mrs. Responsible is completely fagged out, just as if they had gone for a serious work out in the gym. Yeah, I think we should replace the word responsibility with 'workout'!

I decided to take my fitness seriously this year so I have been going to the gym on a regular basis. I started out good, then my attendance slumped for a few months, but I got back into it and have been going strong. I have been working with a personal trainer and going through a routine for development of strength in my upper body.

I remember my first session with him. I actually thought I was going to throw up on the gym floor, pass out and die!

He said we had to work on the muscles in my chest and arms, so he gave me a metal rod to lift without any weights on it. I thought, easy enough, so I lay on my back on the bench and started lifting from my chest level, up in the air, and back again to my chest. After doing this a few times, he had to come to my rescue and help me lift the rod as I could lift no further. My arms were no longer responding to the signals from my brain telling them to lift! I felt so embarrassed as there were other men in the gym lifting rods with 15kg weights or more on either side. He said to me, "Ola man we need to work those muscles until they are tired, worn out and their only response will be to grow so that they can handle the pressure". This he explained was the science to making muscles grow. He also added, "When you are comfortable with one level, we will increase the weight on the rod and tire out those muscles so more growth could take place." After about 3 months, I was amazed at how easy it was for me to lift that rod with weights of 15kg on either side of it. I also began to see a lot of definition in my upper body; I never thought I could achieve this. Amazing! My shame was gone, and I was looking and feeling pretty good with myself.

I can then begin to describe responsibility as the 'workout' required for developing the muscles in different areas of my life that I am accountable for. If I want the muscles in my career to grow, then I must take on more responsibility than I am comfortable with. The same would apply to my relationships, finances, education, time management, energy, resources and more.

The rewards of responsibility do not always look attractive initially, and they sometimes take a while before they show up, but as you keep at it – just like in the gym, eventually you will find yourself handling things that you only thought possible for the mastermind.

I have learnt that responsibility is something that will never go away especially when you reach the age of accountability. I cannot run away or hide from it, I need to rise up to it and face it like a man. I might feel like throwing up, but I must face up to the tasks before me. I might feel ashamed for messing up on my first try, but I must keep going. Pretty soon, my muscles will begin to show, I will be able to easily handle much more than I could previously. My shame will melt away and I will become a standard for others to reference.

No matter how well I have done, if I stop taking on responsibilities, just like my muscles I will begin to grow weaker in my ability to handle things. To keep strong or to handle more, then I must expose myself to even more responsibility.

MONEY MATTERS

"Because of laziness the building decays, And through idleness of hands the house leaks. A feast is made for laughter, And wine makes merry; But money answers everything." – Ecclesiastes 10:18-19

Everyone has much to say about money and there are all kinds of philosophies that transverse all types of culture to advise us on what our relationship with money should be. The view on money goes from one extreme of a life that exalts money above every other thing, to the other, which sees it as the absolute embodiment of all evil, and all types of variant ideas in between. Some would literally sell their family to have more of it on one extreme, and then others would avow to poverty and have none of it. Someone said, "Money can't buy you love!" Another replied, "But it sure can show you a real good time". Whichever way you look at it or whatever your personal view of it, you cannot ignore that money matters.

I have studied the history of money and researched the innovations for its future, so I want to point out a few things.

As you know, money is defined as a means of exchange in the form of coins or banknotes, but before money ever came into being, people still had a means of exchange.

Each person is born with a unique skill and ability to create value, and the value that we create becomes desirable to another who wants access to our creation. Take for instance someone with a skill to sew amazing clothes, at some point their work would be in demand by others. People will spend considerable time creating value. So, the tailor will stay in his shop all day creating outfits instead of going to the farm to plant his seeds. The farmer on the other hand spends all day on the farm and is not able to sew his breeches. They each need the value that the other has created, but each need must occur at the same time as that of the other to make the coincidence right for the exchange of their products. To cut the long story short, money was introduced as a means to represent the value each person had created and the means to exchange that value.

I have changed my thinking around money and I see it as a means to represent the value that I have created. Just like the level of my honesty will represent the value of my integrity, so the level of my money will represent the value of my productivity. Consultants seek to help organizations to be more productive and efficient as a means to increase their profitability. The increase of their money is directly proportional to the level of their productivity and efficiency in the way they do business.

If I am not seeing a reward of the value I possess – monetary or otherwise, then something is definitely wrong. It may mean I am not being productive.

To be productive I need access to resources that my skill can turn into value-product. The farmer needs access to land and seed to produce value. The tailor needs access to material, thread and needle to produce value. The author needs access to pen and paper to produce value.

When I understood this, it really drove home a point I always wondered about – SLAVERY & POVERTY ARE CLOSELY KNIT! Nelson Mandela was quoted as saying, "Money won't create success, the freedom to make it will".

If I take away your access to your abilities and the resources you need to produce value for yourself, then I have enslaved you. If I have enslaved you, then I have made you poor (unproductive or unable to exchange value). Slavery can be a physical confinement where the slave is held in chains and not able to produce for themselves but for others. However, there is also the slavery of a mental confinement where the slave cannot recognise their ability nor identify their resources, and they fight against the idea of owning any measure of their value. Ignorance is slavery; laziness is slavery.

If I am free, then I should have access to my ability and resource. If I have access to ability and resource, then I should be productive. If I am productive, then I should have enough value to exchange. When I exchange value, then I will have more money.

I have learnt that money matters, because my value matters. The 17th Century writer Jonathan Swift said, "A wise man should have money in his head, but not in his heart".

THE HUMAN TOUCH

"To be rich in friends is to be poor in nothing." – Lilian Whiting

Have you heard of the Midas touch? You probably remember the song by the group Midnight Star. According to Greek mythology, he was a king who ruled in the country of Phrygia in the region of Asia Minor. He lived in luxury in a great castle with his beloved daughter. He thought that his greatest happiness was from the abundance of material things he possessed, especially his gold.

At a certain time, Midas showed kindness to a companion of the god of wine, Dionyssus. He was promised that he would get one wish for his kindness. Midas was resolute that his desire was for anything he touched to turn to gold. The next morning, he found that his table turned to gold when he touched it, so he went around his palace touching everything. After a while, he tried to eat but his food turned to gold. Immediately he began to fear that the thing he thought a blessing had actually become a curse. His daughter then walked in to greet him and when they hugged, she turned to a statue of gold. Midas cried out to the god in his predicament and found compassion. He was told to go and wash his hands in the river. His golden touch left him and when he went back to the palace everything that he had touched had returned to its original state.

Sometimes we feel that our greatest riches come from our ability to make things happen and turn a profit from our skills and talents – the works of our hands. Although there is some truth in such thinking, I find a greater truth in this – our true riches are revealed and released in the boundaries of relationships that we have.

A man named Thomas Corley carried out a research over a 5-year period following about 233 very rich people and 128 poor people to uncover their habits. Among other things noted, he found that 80% of wealthy people make happy birthday calls – they value relationships, compared to 17% of the poor. 79% of the wealthy spend 5 hours each month networking with other people – they love meeting new people, compared to 11% of the poor.

Relationships are everything! The value of family, friends, mentors, acquaintances etc. count for far much more than all the gold bullion in the world. Can you think of anything you have achieved outside of a relationship? I laugh at the arrogance of people who stand and declare, "I am a self-made man!" First of all, your Mum and Dad made you (literally), then there was someone who taught you or told you about what you should do. You also had customers or employers that subscribed to whatever goods or services you had to offer. If you could not give birth to yourself, teach yourself all you know, buy from yourself or sell to yourself, then how can

you be a self-made man? We are made emotionally, intellectually, and yes very much financially through the touch of relationships that we have and those that we develop. Relationships are among our most important assets.

Family is the first place where we learn about relationships. In fact, we are born into one. We learn how to touch another human being physically, emotionally, intellectually, materially and otherwise. Being part of a family and then leading one of your own are two things we must strive to maintain or obtain.

Next, we learned to form friendships where we practiced the ability to touch another outside our immediate family. Mohamed Ali said, "Friendship... is not something you learn in school. But if you haven't learned the meaning of friendship, you really haven't learned anything."

Finally, we find that there are relationships that we develop on the job, in business, in our communities, and generally anywhere we spend our time.

I have learnt that having hands that can give the warmth of a human touch would release far more value than the hands with the Midas touch. I must maintain my relationships; I must protect them.

BE ON TIME

"Better three hours too soon than a minute too late." – William Shakespeare

Time is the one resource that once wasted can never be repurchased or replaced. It is probably one of the most important and expensive assets that everyone has. As long as we are alive, we are gifted with the same quantity of time every day – 24 hours. Your time will translate into whatever you spend it on. Time spent studying law will make you a lawyer. Time spent in physical exercise and training will make you fit to be an athlete. Time spent travelling could make you an explorer, and so on. What you spend most of your time doing is a good indicator of what you prioritise or what you want to become.

Coming from an African background, an appointment was generally understood to be in a time window and not necessarily at a specific time. We invented something called the 'African time' with flavours such as Nigerian time, Ghanaian time, Zambian time, Congolese time etc. The whole idea being that if you asked someone to meet you at 2pm, your preparation to leave your house would start at that time. You would have lunch, take a bath, dress up and then leave your house. You would eventually meet up at 4pm (maybe I have slightly exaggerated the scenario).

On the other hand, most of Western Europe has a deep respect for time. In fact, being timely is almost a religion and if you are a late comer you are almost viewed as some kind of heretic. (Again, maybe I exaggerate this slightly).

I remember an incident that happened to me about a year after moving to the United Kingdom. I had been living with my sister and her husband while studying for my Masters. When I finished my course, I was looking for a place of my own to rent. I had to look for a very affordable one-room accommodation. These were called bedsits – your bed, kitchen and bathroom were all in one room. I found the perfect place at a reasonable price and the landlord set up a meeting with me so we could sign the contract and he would collect my deposit. We were to meet at 1pm on the day of exchange, but I lingered trying to gather enough cash for my deposit. At 1.05pm I finally went to the cash point to withdraw the rest of the money and started heading to our rendezvous. I called him to say I was on my way. He was absolutely livid and after giving me an earful he said he was leaving. He told me not to contact him again as he had lost interest in giving me the room. I apologised, pleaded and tried to explain, but he retorted, "If you could not make a simple appointment, I have no trust that you would pay my rent on time". He said he did not want the hassle of dealing with me. I found another place a couple of days later and the deal looked too good to be true. The property was advertised as "Landlord who is constantly travelling looking for a house sitter". The amount for the rent was next to nothing. I quickly made my way on time to see this landlord. To cut the long story short, this guy told me that he wanted to be my sex slave and I should be his master. I could not believe my ears, and I can't remember how I was able to leave that property politely. Once I got out of there I was shaken and remained quite astonished for a few days. I called back the first landlord to see if he had forgiven and forgotten our little incident, but he was still adamant that he wanted nothing to do with me. He made it clear that he would get the police involved if I persisted to call him again, as he would consider that to be harassment.

No one had to speak another word to me about the value of being on time. I learnt that day that time is important. I needed to be on time, and I needed to respect other people's time. If people regarded their time that much, then I also needed to revisit how much I valued my own time. To be on time shows preparation for a task, consideration for others, accommodation of eventualities, and is key to the optimisation of the 24 hours we have all been given. Showing up on time could be crucial in saving a life, catching a flight, or sealing a deal. I made an adjustment regarding appointments I had arranged or agreed to such that if for any reason I were to be running late for that appointment, I would contact the person I was to meet way in advance to explain my circumstances and also to give them enough notice to decide what they needed to do next.

I have since become a better manager of my time and I can see the wisdom and rewards of being on time always.

DISCIPLINE

"In reading the lives of great men, I found that the first victory they won was over themselves... self-discipline with all of them came first."
– Harry S Truman

Discipline is defined in the Oxford dictionary as "The practice of training people to obey rules or a code of behaviour, using punishment to correct disobedience." The early appearance of the word in Latin 'disciplina' means Instruction.

I went to a military secondary school in Nigeria which was run by soldiers and civilians. Discipline was a big thing in the army and it was one of our watch-words as students of this institution. The focus of the word was always brought home to us leaning more towards the punishment side rather than the instruction.

Our military instructors were always happy to 'discipline' anyone stepping out of bounds. I remember at the time of lessons if someone interrupted the class while the teacher's back was turned, he would ask "who interrupted my class?" If no one owned up, the whole class would then be punished. Sometimes we got punished and were not even sure of the reasons why, but we had to accept it as part of being disciplined.

In 1985, my first year in secondary school, there was a military coup which ousted a civilian government branded as being corrupt. One of the measures introduced to tackle the corruption and indiscipline prevalent in the nation was the introduction of a scheme called "War Against Indiscipline - WAI". The military government (*led by General Muhammadu Buhari and his deputy General Tunde Idiagbon*) said we needed to tackle indiscipline being one of the ills of our society. There was a brigade set up to monitor adherence to law and order, and to fish out and punish those that behaved disorderly. This brigade put the fear of God in the hearts of many Nigerians who then began to line up with a semblance of order. One became careful not to step out of line for fear of the consequences. Again this reinforced the punishment more than the training and Instruction. After that particular government was ousted for another one with a different policy, people soon found their way back to the disorder that seemed more familiar to them. I realised in those years that discipline could be forced upon you to modify your habits temporarily or you could decide to take it upon yourself for a more permanent change.

There is a lot of wisdom in any type of discipline but it must clearly offer both the instruction and then the punishment of disobedience to those instructions. There is a reason for discipline in any system be it external – national, regional, companywide, family – or internal i.e. yourself. The rules and code of behaviour when well thought through help to protect people in the system from various risk and possible accidents. If there were no rules for driving on the roads, think about the chaos and loss of life that would ensue. If there were no regulations for banking, how many people would be ripped off of their hard earned cash.

My experiences back in secondary school began to make sense, I did not think it fair to be punished when the offender was hiding in our midst, but the reality is that the discipline in a system is the joint responsibility of everyone. There were many codes of practice that were broken in the financial industry in the years leading up to the 2008 global recession. Many were aware of it yet they never called it out. The consequences of those actions ended up affecting us all.

On a personal level, a refusal to apply discipline to just one area of your life like how you manage your time, money or desires could be the thing that –if you don't call out – has the potential to sabotage your personal progress in any sphere of your endeavours. The word disciple made popular by the followers of Christ, means to be a learner. Subjecting yourself to a discipline will make you a disciple. Looking at discipline from a learning perspective gave it a whole new meaning to me for one can only improve for the better when one has learnt.

I have learnt that I must allow myself to be subject to the discipline of external systems that I am a part of – not passively, but actively contributing to it; while also being in control of my own personal system bringing discipline to myself. I must learn in the areas I need to improve, but also not let myself off the hook for the punishments I need to endure in order to build the proper discipline into my life.

ORDER

"Some people regard discipline as a chore. For me, it is a kind of order that sets me free to fly." – **Julie Andrews**

As a child I was intrigued by TV shows that depicted a court setting and my favourite scenes were of the Judge hitting his gavel on the table and shouting, "Order! Order in the court!" Anyone who persisted with disorderly conduct was charged with contempt of court. The judge would at best declare a fine or at worst dish out a jail sentence to that individual who would then be taken away by the court bailiff.

I wondered why this thing called order was so important that one could acquire such harsh penalties for not observing it. Order can be defined as: The disposition of things following one after another, as in space or time; succession or sequence: E.g. the names were listed in alphabetical order. Or, a condition in which each thing is properly disposed with reference to other things and to its purpose; methodical or harmonious arrangement: e.g. you must try to give order to your life.

Everything in life has some kind of methodical arrangement for its purpose to be fulfilled, and a proper sequence in which that arrangement should come together. Take for instance plants – their purpose is to grow and bear some kind of fruit. First, let's talk about the conditions to facilitate growth. Remember the scientific experiment of trying to grow beans back in school? We needed the bean seed, soil, water, light, and atmosphere (air). All these had to be arranged in a methodical order for the purpose of growth to happen. The seed goes in the soil, then it is watered , then daylight rises on it and air is available in the atmosphere. If any one factor were missing, it would affect the arrangement and sequence. In other words, it would disrupt the order. The seed would only grow for a while but eventually it would die. In the same vein, if any one of the factors were applied to the seed out of the proper sequence, the seed would likely die. Adding water first, then light and air would make the seed grow only for a little while, but without the soil coming first in the sequence, the seed would struggle to survive.

Applying this principle to other areas of life, you will agree that a lack of order is detrimental to any individual or society. The most progressive nations on earth are known for their law and order. The poorest, under-developed nations are known for their disorder.

One of the questions I struggled with was "how do I create order in my life?" There were times I got it right, but at other times I was a complete mess. Looking again at the analogy of the seed, even though I had all the conditions right, and I arranged them in proper sequence, what I had done could not be left as a one-off exercise. If I did not continue to water the seed regularly, if the sun did not shine daily, if the ground and atmosphere were not constantly there, then even though I had arranged things right, I still would not get the results of order as expected.

When I started going to the gym regularly, I would see some men looking like the Incredible Hulk. I could lift some of the weights they were lifting at least once, but it did not transform me right then. My personal trainer told me I needed to do the reps (repetitions) of lifting the weight over a period of time to get their results. This all made sense, and it shouted out to me that if I were going to create order in my life, I needed to stick to a routine.

Sometimes, my wife and I are terribly exhausted at the end of a working day and trying to maintain some semblance of order in our busy lives is difficult. I had to ask my mum the other day, however did you cope with so many children? It's two of us against our son in my home and we still feel overrun, yet it was many of us against you. How on earth did you do it? She answered, "I had to maintain a routine like we were in a military camp."

Routines are powerful and it is the chief way that the human body and mind learns and grows. If I tidied up my kitchen today and restored order in my home, it would not stay like that all week. By the next day after my dinner, the state of the kitchen would be alarming. I would have to clean it up again. Routine is what helps us to maintain order. After a while, the routine becomes such a part of us that it is no longer much of an effort to do it. Like brushing our teeth every morning. It doesn't feel like a chore, and if we don't do it, we feel like something is wrong. Let's not even talk about the bad breath that follows.

I have learnt the importance of bringing order into every area of my life so my best results can come out of those areas. I have also learnt to follow routines to ensure that my order is maintained.

VALUES

"Try not to become a man of success, but rather try to become a man of value."
– Albert Einstein

So what are values? They can be defined as principles or standards of behaviour; one's judgment of what is important in life. Other synonyms used to describe values are principles, ethics, morals, standards, and rules of conduct. The word is also used to describe the worth, estimate or price of a thing.

People that stick to a certain code of living eventually become known for those things they have stuck to. Even though others may not subscribe to their manner of life, at some point, the consistency of their behaviour will make them notable. Eventually, what they value will make them valuable. But just like any other precious thing, your values will be tried and tested as gold or silver is tried in a furnace. Usually the furnace that tests the value of men is the conversation that people begin to hold about them. There will be those that inflate your values and others who will berate them, both are just as injurious because the same one that sings 'Hosanna!' today will also chorus 'Crucify him!' tomorrow. Either cry has the potential to distract you from what you hold on to.

Once you have been noted as a person with values, those values will begin to attract notoriety and success to your life. Then the next trial comes, and this one is probably the most insidious of the attacks you would face. It is the offer of great fame, power, and riches with a very small sprinkle of compromise to your values.

Think about the great activists, sports personalities, religious leaders etc. that had an excellent set of values. They then became famous and after a while you hear about how they were embroiled in one scandal or another. Upon further consideration of their plight, you will find that the compromise of some of their key values is what got them into that mess. Conversely, there are great personalities who rose to a place of great influence, but who also maintained their set of values and would not compromise. We hail them as true heroes.

So what are your values? What are those things that you believe and hold on to? The things that guide the way you live? As the saying goes, "if you don't stand for something, you will fall for anything". It is the things that we stand for that guarantee our stability in tough times so that we do not fall when the pressures come.

Does your value set include; love, faith, trust, commitment, obedience, generosity, responsibility, accountability, integrity, respect, hard work, honesty, sincerity, punctuality, truth, family, health, moderation, discipline, care for others, justice, forgiveness, honour, integrity?

I have learnt that I must from time to time revisit the basis for my values and never exchange my value-set for any form of fame, notoriety, power or riches. Values will attract all those things but staying true to my values will help me to maintain them in the right balance that is needed.

REGRETS

"Never look back unless you are planning to go that way."
– Henry D. Thoreau

Everyone makes bad decisions from time to time. Some of those decisions cause us to regret the actions that we took or did not take. For me to regret, I must recall the thing I have done. I somehow make a journey back into my past and closely watch the steps that led up to my actions. I relive that experience for a very brief moment of time. The problem is that the brevity of my flashback triggers emotions that linger possibly for days.

No matter what I do to change the past, it doesn't budge. Sometimes I try to deny it, but the record still remains. I try to explain it away, but I am still left with a nagging complaint. I paint over it, but it still has a taint that won't cover. What can be done to fix my past? How can I resolve my regret? We have all kinds of fantasies about time travel, going back to fix the past so that we can erase some part of our present or future and make it more bearable. But the truth is that once an event has occurred, it is past and nothing can be done to change it. The only reasonable way to deal with the past and regret is to learn from it, and then leave it where it belongs, behind you. There is no point crying over spilt milk.

Have you ever been on a journey with a friend and for some reason you missed a turn that caused your journey to be extended by a few extra hours? You don't stop there and cry about it or relive it or blame each other for it. You try to keep moving until you get back on track and eventually get to your destination. Bad decisions can make it seem like we have wasted years of our life, yet living in regret hinders us from making the adjustment to reroute to our destination.

"No matter how far off you've gone from the mark,

There is still time to get back on track,

Don't waste that season analysing your past,

Take up the reason to get to your future fast."

I have seen that a past – no matter how colourful or colourless it was – has no bearing on what the future could hold. I have seen men come from a past of great depravity yet end up in a place of abundance. There were people who were told that they can't because of what they had done, yet they ended up achieving what was thought impossible.

What we are today is a sum total of decisions that we made in the past. If I keep reliving my regrets, I am wasting time recounting decisions that did not help me, thus creating a future that will produce the same results of disappointment. However, if I take lessons from my past and focus on changing what I am doing in my present, then I am guaranteeing a future with a better outcome.

There are two powerful capacities that the human mind possesses. One is to remember (go back to the past) and the other is to imagine (look into the future). These abilities are always used now (in the present). What I remember could help or hinder me in my today, but what I imagine could open up a new door into a greater tomorrow.

Someone said the future belongs to the dreamer. If I spend all my time living in regret, I use up all my mental capacity on the past which cannot be changed; I deny myself the experiences of the present which must be engaged, and I limit my capacity for imagining a future in which I am advantaged.

I have learnt that the only permission that my regrets have to hold me back is the permission I give it when I keep revisiting my past. I have learnt to enjoy the experiences of my present, applying the learning from the past to make it better. I am using the power of my imagination over the power of my memory to see a future that has endless possibility.

FORGIVENESS

"We must develop and maintain the capacity to forgive. He who is devoid of the power to forgive is devoid of the power to love. There is some good in the worst of us and some evil in the best of us. When we discover this, we are less prone to hate our enemies." – **Martin Luther King, Jr.**

"As I walked out the door toward the gate that would lead to my freedom, I knew if I didn't leave my bitterness and hatred behind, I'd still be in prison." – **Nelson Mandela**

There is a great explanation of forgiveness I found on Wikipedia and it says, "Forgiveness is the intentional and voluntary process by which a victim undergoes a change in feelings and attitude regarding an offense, let's go of negative emotions such as vengefulness, with an increased ability to wish the offender well. Forgiveness is different from condoning (*failing to see the action as wrong and in need of forgiveness*), excusing (*not holding the offender as responsible for the action*), pardoning (*granted by a representative of society, such as a judge*), forgetting (*removing awareness of the offense from consciousness*), and reconciliation (*restoration of a relationship*). In certain contexts, forgiveness is a legal term for absolving or giving up all claims on account of debt, loan, obligation or other claims."

It is probably one of the greatest needs that one man will have from another, and the most urgent thing that one should give to another. The very nature of the word 'For' 'Giving' lets me know that it's meant to be given; it's not 'For' 'Keeping'.

The concept of forgiveness is strongly rooted in all the major world religions of the east and west, and Christianity particularly elaborates on the importance of forgiveness that one receives from God and also gives to their fellow man - free of charge. It also teaches that forgiveness is more important for the giver than the receiver of it.

Social and medical sciences have studied the concept of forgiveness and its effect on the individual and their community. Some research results on forgiveness published in the Harvard review on health reveal that mentally nursing a grudge puts your body through the same strains as a major stressful event. One study found a link between forgiving someone for a betrayal and improvements in blood pressure and heart rate, and a decreased workload for the heart. A 2004 study showed that women who were able to forgive their spouses and feel benevolent toward them resolved conflicts more effectively. A small study on people with chronic back pain found that those who practiced meditation focusing on converting anger to compassion felt less pain and anxiety than those who received regular care. One survey showed that people who talk about forgiveness during psychotherapy sessions experience greater improvements than those who don't.

I remember some very painful moments in my life where I was deeply hurt by people I loved and trusted. I felt a kind of pain that I never dreamed possible; it was shocking, crippling and very traumatic. I remember crying to a close friend, and asking the question, "why did they do this to me?" – I was very angry with my offenders but even angrier with myself for letting them treat me the way they did – his answer shook me! He said "why not you?", he went on to explain that no one was better than anyone else and all men are so flawed that it is unrealistic to expect they would not hurt one another. His final point was, it's not what happened to you that's important but how you deal with what happened.

It was a hard lesson to swallow, but I knew it was true and if I were to be healed of my pain, I must forgive. It is very true that the one who holds a grudge puts their body through the strains of the same traumatic event over and over again. I lived and re-lived my pain for months, but the wisdom of my friend eventually prevailed. I forgave, I let it go! It was like a heavy burden was taken off my heart and body. I felt free to live again and rebuild my life, I stopped talking about it and trying to get people on my side. When you forgive someone, you make yourself — rather than the person who hurt you — responsible for your happiness.

Sometimes we acknowledge the virtues of forgiveness and maybe even preach it to people that have been hurt, but it is a totally different proposition when we are hurt. Then, we are not so quick to practice what we preach. I have learnt that forgiveness is 'for' me to 'give' to others as well as to myself. People will always do things that will hurt, knowingly or unknowingly, so I will not live in denial of the nature of men but will be quick to mitigate the curve balls that they throw at me by forgiving, then taking positive action.

BE THANKFUL

"Cultivate the attitude of being grateful for every good thing that comes to you, and to give thanks continuously. And because all things have contributed to your advancement, you should include all things in your gratitude."
– Ralph Waldo Emerson

One of the things I remember being reprimanded for as a child – especially when I was given something – was for not saying thank you. It was good manners to say please when you asked for something and thank you after you received it. Some call it the attitude of gratitude, others call it being appreciative but we all seem to agree it is an important code of conduct for the sane individual.

There is the story of the man who had no shoes and he was very sad until he came across the man who had no feet. This made him change his mind and he was thankful for the feet that he had. It is a sad reality of the human nature that we hardly take stock of the benefits we have until we come across another who lacks it. Is this the only way that we should be prompted to be thankful?

I like the meaning of the word 'appreciation' – the act of estimating the qualities of things and giving them their proper value. To me this is the real purpose of being thankful. So rather than wait to see the misfortunes of others or hear about them before I am thankful, I daily take stock of what I have and ensure that I ascribe to them the proper value they deserve. To be thankful is to constantly be aware of the purpose and value of the things that I have.

In that case, I am thankful for being alive and well!

I am thankful for my family –
father, mother, siblings, cousins, uncles and aunties.

I am thankful for my wife.

I am thankful for my children.

I am thankful for my friends –
the good, bad and ugly!

I am thankful for my teachers –
then and now.

I am thankful for my education.

I am thankful for my gifts and talents.

I am thankful for my job and career.

I am thankful for my enemies.

I am thankful for my mistakes –
and what I learned from them.

I am thankful for my successes.

I am thankful for my church family.

I am thankful for my mentors.

I am thankful for what I have.

I am thankful for what I lack.

I am thankful for the places I have visited.

I am thankful for where I live.

I am thankful for my provisions –
food, clothing and shelter.

I am thankful for my opportunities.

I am thankful for my possibilities.

I am thankful for favour.

I am thankful for when doors open.

I am thankful for when they shut.

I am thankful for the good days.

I am thankful for the bad ones too.

I am thankful for my purpose.

I am thankful for age 40.

I am thankful for today.

I am thankful for my future!

I have learnt that I should be thankful, grateful, and appreciative of all things at all times. This is the way I keep taking stock and maintaining my perspective on their purpose in my life.

CREATE THE MOOD

"Act the way you want to feel" – Gretchen Rubin

Moods are funny things; they are a reflection of the way we are feeling. That feeling has a huge impact on the way we will perform in whatever thing we have to do. Have you ever been accused of being moody? I have, at different stages of my life. As a child they told me I complained too much, my aunty used to call me the commissioner of complaint. I kind of liked the title because at least I was a commissioner, LOL! Over the years I have lived through good moods, bad moods, anxious moods, sad moods, happy moods, angry moods and so on. And then, there are the mood swings. Just like a roller coaster ride they take you up and down, round and round and from side to side.

So what on earth does one do about their moods? I always thought that moods were all powerful and when they were triggered by some event, then just like a pack of stacked cards everything in me would fall under the sway of that mood. Well I am glad my thinking was wrong!

Bob Marley sang a song with the opening lyrics, "Turn your lights down low…" he was singing about creating another kind of mood. Men trying to grasp the attention of the opposite sex always want to do things that create the right mood; purposefully taking actions to design a certain kind of atmosphere. I can also think of people that do irritating things almost purposefully to get on one's nerves. I find that apart from random things happening to bring a mood on, people can also take action to influence a mood too. I have learnt that instead of falling prey to the moods that arise due to circumstances, or the devices of other people, I can create my own moods.

Here are a few simple ways I have done this:

Talking to myself – especially when I feel fearful and discouraged. I talk myself out of that negative feeling.

Singing – even though I don't have a great voice, I can sing like a maestro in the shower. A good song moves me into the atmosphere of the lyrics of that song.

Dancing – this is a great mood lifter. Recently my son started asking for my wife and I to dance with him. We would hold hands and do the 'ring-a ring-a roses' dance, LOL! What an awesome feeling.

Praying – calling on the Almighty One in time of difficulty brings hope in the place of despair.

Walking – I take a good long walk and it has a way of unwinding the pent up frustrations on my mind.

Sharing – the act of taking what you have and giving part of it to another in need lifts up the soul to tremendous heights.

Shouting – find somewhere to go and have a good shout for no reason. E.g. like watching a football game.

Playing a game – there are all kinds of games to play, but I find that physical games with other people are the best.

I must however point out that when you try to change from one mood to another, especially from a bad one to a good one, everything in you tends to feel awkward, like you are pretending to bring on something that is not real. Well you have to ignore that thinking because if you don't give in to it, suddenly your mood will change and you will truly be swinging in a pretty good mood.

Sports persons know this; they have to maintain a positive attitude even when they are losing a game. They employ psychologists that work with them to train them on managing their moods. Once their moods are under control, then their performance can be optimized. I have decided not to allow foul moods to hold me back from performing at my best. I can manage my moods and sway them rather than letting them sway me.

RECAPTURE THE QUALITIES OF YOUR INNER CHILD

"So, like a forgotten fire, a childhood can always flare up again within us"
– Gaston Bachelard

As I watch my son grow I realize how beautiful children are; the innocence, purity, enthusiasm, trust, love, joy and laughter, hope, boldness, confidence, excitement at new things, acceptance of everyone, telling things as it is and so on. Watching him and other children bring back fond memories of the joy I once had when I was a child.

My older brother wrote a poem and a few lines in it really caught my attention and they have stayed with me.

"Every child is pure energy,

Energy looking for direction,

Environment possesses positive direction,

Environment possesses negative direction."

– Kayo Opebiyi

It is so true that as a child grows, whatever qualities they have begin to be moulded and influenced by the environment that they find themselves in. Before long that sweet child could either become even more charming or transformed into something really menacing. Life throws so much in the mix that the child is forced to come to grips with as they grow. Parents are meant to soften those punches but sometimes for whatever reason, they could have been absent or even when they were present, they missed out on their duty of care.

The child soon finds out that Santa is not real! Adults lie too, promises are sometimes broken, the world is not a bed of roses, people can be unkind and hurtful, fears and dangers are becoming more real and the list could go on.

Somewhere along the line those beautiful qualities of that child begin to be readjusted, rationalized and sometimes even disappear. The once hopeful and joyous child could soon become a cynical young man or woman just like the people that influenced them.

I remember back in secondary school, one of my teachers decided to punish me for a perceived wrong. He beat me so hard with a cane, striking me all over my body and when he was done I could see black and blue marks under my skin. Needless to say my father got involved and reported this to the authorities. But that experience affected me for years and took away a certain confidence I had up until that point. My experience was bad, but there are children who have been through much worse.

Looking at society and attempting to come to grips with the evil that men act out, then trying to reconcile that with the fact that they were once an embodiment of those great qualities of a child is a very hard thing to do. The events that shaped them may have been outside their control at the time they were young and that is very understandable, however, if it were to be tried in a court of law, those excuses would not stand. Once you are deemed to have passed the age of accountability and are in a sound state of mind, it is expected that you have properly thought through the consequences of your own actions.

Thinking about these things made me reflect on my life and question everything that I had been taught and exposed to. Had I lost all the admirable qualities of my inner child? Am I on the right path or have I continued down a wrong road? Have I been influenced in the right way or in the wrong way? We must have a willingness to challenge, research, relearn, realign and change in any area of our lives where we discover that we have got it wrong.

I have learnt to ask myself, "What great qualities of my inner child have I lost?" "Why did I lose them?" "How can I recapture them?" I will not let the negative environment rob me of living that great life that I had a promise of when I was a child. I will not let the circumstances and the mistakes of others keep me in a dark corner locked down from my greatest possibilities. I will recapture the qualities of my inner child, I will allow that pure energy to come out and be expressed!

I KEPT QUIET

"The Ultimate tragedy is not the oppression and cruelty by the bad people but silence over that by the good people…in the end, we will remember not the words of our enemies, but the silence of our friends"
– Martin Luther King Jnr

My schooling years in Nigeria were fun, but at the same time they put the fear of God in me. I went to a military secondary school and the style of teaching was such that when the teachers asked a question, everyone was expected to know the answer. If you did not know the answer, all I can say is God help you! There was a particular maths teacher who traumatized us. We would see him marching down the corridors like a man who had just lost something very precious and was frantically searching for it. He would bolt into the class and then pointing his finger at a random student he would shout "You, 7 times 8!" he would wait for all of 2 seconds for an answer and if he didn't get one he would ask that student to come out and kneel down in front of the class, he would then go on the next random student asking the next random question from the multiplication table and so on.

This made the students very wary of speaking up in the class as you could get into trouble for not knowing. I guess his methods were to scare us and jolt us into doing our assignments and reading our notes so that we would be able to answer questions that came up suddenly.

At those times I kept as quiet and still as I possibly could because I did not know the answers and I did not want to get picked on.

I found that keeping quiet was a kind of defence or protection mechanism just like a small creature would do trying to avoid the attention of its predators.

Life would sometimes throw up sudden random questions that it perhaps expects us to answer. The unexpected death of a loved one occurs, then came the questions, but answers were hard to find so I kept quiet. Relationships were tried due to reasons beyond control, cracks began to show and breakups were inevitable yet I kept quiet. All hell broke loose on the job, accusations flying and confidence diving, yet I kept quiet. A good friend is going through a very rough patch and needs great amounts of time and resources to get out of it, yet I kept quiet. Someone is being abused and the thought that it might really be happening is too hard to handle, so I kept quiet.

I kept quiet because I did not know the answer. I kept quiet because I felt hurt by the actions of others against me. I kept quiet because I did not know how to help. I kept quiet because I did not have enough to give. I kept quiet because I was discouraged. I kept quiet because I had messed up badly and was too ashamed to acknowledge it. I kept quiet because I did not want my situation to be exposed. I kept quiet because I was so scared. I kept quiet because the challenge looked too great to surmount.

Martin Luther King Jnr said "The Ultimate tragedy is not the oppression and cruelty by the bad people but silence over that by the good people…in the end, we will remember not the words of our enemies, but the silence of our friends". Our silence can be quite damning to us and the ones we love or those to whom we have a duty of care.

One day the maths teacher came into the class and in his usual manner he pointed at a particular student and blurted out "You, 9 times 12!" that day an answer came back "108!" again he asked him "6 times 8!" the answer came back too! This went on for a while then all of a sudden the students that were quiet and timid began to sit up wide eyed watching this spectacle. Before long, we all began to cheer and clap, much to the displeasure of the teacher. Someone did it, someone had a go, someone stood up to it; someone gave an answer!

I look back over the years and ponder the points in my life where I kept quiet; I wish I could have spoken up. However, coming back to the present, I have learnt to speak up even in the most difficult of circumstances, I have learnt to speak up and say I don't know. I have learnt to speak up and say I made a mistake. I have learnt to speak up for another going through pain. I have learnt that there is somebody somewhere going through what I am going through who has found the courage to speak up; I should listen to what they say and draw strength from them.

PREPARATION

"Before anything else, preparation is the key to success."
– Alexander Graham Bell

Good things usually come well packaged and you have to open up the layers of the wrappers that cover them to get to the substance inside. I remember once being convinced to eat a clementine without peeling the outer cover. All I can say is that it was a very bitter-sweet experience and one that I will not be repeating again.

You cannot use a gift to its full potential when it is wrapped up. You must get rid of all the outer coating to enjoy the essence of the actual product on the inside.

I love the etymology (derivation of a word) of PREPARE. It is made up of two words, PRE – which means 'before', and PARE – which means 'to cut off the outer coating'. Although the dictionary defines prepare as "To put in proper condition or readiness", I do like to describe it as "Cut off the outer coating before…" So, to prepare a meal you would have to cut off the outer packaging of your ingredients before you can get it ready.

As the saying goes, "If you fail to plan, you plan to fail." Planning and preparation go hand in hand, they seem very similar but they are not the same. I planned to travel to the USA at the beginning of the year, so I booked a flight and hotel accommodation, then packed my bags a few days before the trip, booked a taxi to get to the airport and then showed up at my terminal on the day of my departure.

The plan was to travel to the USA, but the preparation was all the other stuff I did to make it happen.

Thoughts, ideas, opportunities, possibilities and plans all present themselves to us, encouraging us to take some kind of action with them to better our lives. There has to be some form of preparation before we can execute those things. Taking action on them without properly preparing may lead to some good results, but just like the clementine, there may be more unpleasant circumstance surrounding the outcome.

I usually think of it this way: any opportunity that presents itself to me is a 'present'. That means it is wrapped up. In order for me to benefit from it, I must 'cut off the outer coating before…' I can make good use of it. There is some level of preparation I must make towards that opportunity.

Ideas and opportunities can sometime be confusing and create contradictions in your mind. "Should I relocate?" "Do I marry that person?" "Can I accomplish this thing that no one has ever done before?"

Those questions, contradictions, confusions, pain points and everything else that come with the idea are all wrappers. It is preparation that will help you to unravel the outer coverings to get to the substance inside, then you are able to clearly see if the substance is good for you or not.

I want to start a business, but I must cut off the outer covering of how to do it before I can start. Asking questions and getting answers to them is the great pair of scissors to cut through the covering surrounding your opportunity. The more you know about it, the more you will be able to get ready for it.

As I look back on my journey through life, I can see the areas where I failed to prepare and the pains that accompanied them, but I also see the experiences that were largely pleasant because I properly planned for them. It was all kind of hit and miss back then, but now I have learnt to use my scissors of preparation more and more so that I have more days of a hit rather than a miss.

MAKING
DECISIONS

"In any moment of decision, the best thing you can do is the right thing, the next best thing is the wrong thing, and the worst thing you can do is nothing."
– Theodore Roosevelt

We are faced with hundreds of decisions every day and they all line up one after the other waiting for an answer. Have you ever been in a restaurant being asked what you wanted to drink? You said water and expected your request to be fulfilled, instead you got more questions, "from the tap or bottled?" "Still or sparkling?" "With ice or without?" at this point you wanted to scream, "Just get me some water to drink!"

It is because we are faced with so many choices that we have to make a decision as to which choice we should go with. Making a decision is simply making a choice for one thing out of a host of other things.

The concept is very simple, yet I found that it was a big struggle for me. Some years back, while waiting for an appointment I was flipping through a book titled 'On Penalties' I happened to stumble across this passage, "The human spirit may crave freedom, but it recoils from choice. To commit to one option – to live with a certain person rather than another, say, or to go to this New Year's Eve party and not that one – is to confront the irreversibility of time. In this sense, to make a choice in life is to recognize the inevitability of death. That's why we procrastinate, or attempt to suspend the moment of decision, for as long as we can." This made so much sense to me and helped me to understand the unexplained struggles I had felt about making decisions.

Time is of the essence when we talk about making decisions, and even though decision-making looks like a complex mesh of permutations and combinations of options to choose from, it all boils down to making one choice at one particular point in time. You might have a hundred more choices to make based on that one choice, but they will occur one after the other even though in very rapid succession.

Have you noticed that even in the movies, the hero has to make a choice between saving their loved one and disarming the explosive device? They are only given a very limited time by the villain to make that decision. To remain undecided or to postpone a decision for longer than necessary is probably worse than making a bad decision. Why is this so? Well if I make a bad decision, I can always learn from the experience and retrace my steps to make better ones next time. If I don't make a decision, time keeps racing and the opportunity to make that choice passes by, so I would have lost both my time and my choice.

No matter how many options we are faced with, in the final analysis we will always be left with the two best things to do for that particular point in time.

Left or right, up or down, on or off, good or bad, forward or backward, leave or stay, speak or remain silent. A decision needs to be made; one thing needs to be chosen in order to progress.

I think of decision making like walking. In order to walk, first you must stand up on your two feet – this is where you take full responsibility for sifting out all your choices and crystalizing your thoughts to identify the two best options. Next, you must put one foot in front of the other – this is where you make the choice for what you think is best, and you leave the other behind. You may fall the first few steps you try to make, but just like a child, you must get up and keep trying and the more you do it, the easier it will become. The next thing then is to repeat the process again, putting one foot in front of the other in quick successions of time and thus make progress.

To be indecisive is to sit where you are overwhelmed by the myriad of choices to make, or, to come to a point of standing, but then not making the choice to put one thing before the other thus allowing time to slowly pass you by as you are left on the same spot.

So how do I become better at making decisions? I have learnt to do this by seeking out enough information on the choices I have to make, getting the counsel and advice of others, following my gut feeling, imagining the outcomes of my decision, being proactive by just doing something, and finally using a combination of all the methods mentioned.

LANGUAGE AND CULTURE

"If you talk to a man in a language he understands, that goes to his head. If you talk to him in his own language, that goes to his heart." – **Nelson Mandela**

Have you ever been in a situation where you tried to communicate, saying the right words yet it was evident that you stuck out like a sore thumb and were identified as not belonging in that place? Everything looked good on the outside but all went wrong when you opened your mouth to speak. While growing up I tried to speak my father's dialect, but each time I attempted to, the people I was trying to converse with made fun of me because I did not speak it very well. Eventually, I stopped trying.

I have since found that language goes beyond the ability to articulate words for the purpose of communication. Language is defined as "A body of words and the systems for their use common to a people who are of the same community or nation, the same geographical area, or the same cultural tradition:"

Language is one of the strongest attributes of a culture and is made up of words and expressions that are used to describe the history, knowledge, experiences, thinking and aspirations of that culture.

The one who masters language is the one who is able to master relationship to the culture of that language. I have met a few polyglots (one who is able to speak many languages) and found that they shared certain characteristics. Apart from the fact that they were quite jovial and friendly, they showed a genuine interest in the people they engaged in conversation, and displayed openness to the others' way of life.

Apart from cultures that are bound by geographical or ethnical boundaries where national languages are in place, there are also other forms of cultural expressions. For instance, religion, political persuasion, social status, profession etc., these types of cultures sometimes have a stronger hold that supersedes that of ethnical or national identity. The combination of say religion and nationality can form a culture within a culture that creates some type of super culture.

Every language has a culture it belongs to, but every culture has a language that it subscribes to.

I remember back in university, I was on a campus in a state in northern Nigeria that was predominantly Muslim. A student from another university in the predominantly Christian south of the country happened to be stuck in our city and decided to come to the campus to find refuge. He got to the campus and asked if there were any chess players he could camp with for the night. He was somehow brought to my room, and as we got talking I quizzed him on his strange request to be taken to a chess player rather than one from our southern culture. In his response, he had reckoned that being a southerner and a Christian, he needed to find something that would increase his chances of engaging with a northerner and possibly a Muslim, in his search for a place to stay for the night. He was a great chess player and thought that he would get on with another chess player irrespective of their cultural background.

I now understand that he was trying to use the language of chess, understood by fellow chess players, as a way of breaking down other cultural barriers to engage with another person. Since then, I noticed that this same principle applies to other areas like, which football team one supports, professional experiences, genre of music listened to, types of films watched, interests, hobbies and so on. This secondary culture within a main culture has the potential to break down language and other ethnical-cultural barriers to forge understanding.

I have learnt that in order to communicate on a deeper level with a certain culture, I must go a step further and rather than just learning the words, I actually begin to immerse myself in the context of that culture. What I found was that if I were able to get into the mind-set of the culture, even though I was not fluent with the words of it, my communication was more heartfelt than if I only knew the proper articulation of the language.

VISION

"The most pathetic person in the world is someone who has sight but no vision."
– Helen Keller

Great people are always described as visionary. They accomplish what others think impossible, and keep going in spite of all the odds stacked up against them. They change the way the world around them thinks, and redefine new ways of doing things. They are usually described as innovators, inventors, leaders, communicators, imaginative, energetic, focused and more.

There are three broad meanings under which the word vision lies. First, is the ability of sensing with the eyes; second, is the imaginative conception or anticipation of that which will or may come to be; third, is an experience in which a person, thing or event appears to one's mind, often under the influence of a divine or other agency.

However you look at it, vision is all about seeing. Seeing by physical, mental or spiritual means. I have always wondered why majority of people who have eyes are not described as visionary. Surely, if I have eyes, I must have vision? If that is not the case then, how do I actually begin to develop the ability to have meaningful vision?

The way our eyes have been set in our head limit our ability to only seeing what is directly in front of us. If I wanted to see what was behind me, I would have to turn and face that direction. My physical vision is best suited for the things that lie ahead of me and this is also true for all other types of vision.

When driving on the highway, a driver watches the road ahead being mindful of other vehicles and stationary objects as he approaches them. If another driver in front of him swerves or breaks suddenly, because he was watching, chances are he will react quickly to avoid an accident. If however he was distracted by looking into his rear-view mirror or talking to the person next to him in the passenger's seat, he might end up in a collision.

Another thing to note is that the driver's level of attention to what lies ahead is informed by his level of acceptance of responsibility for what he is carrying. If the driver is conscious of the importance of his life, the lives of others in the vehicle and indeed the value of the vehicle itself, he would be more attentive to what might happen next. So we can say that the size of the responsibility he is willing to accept will determine the size and importance of the vision he is open to receive.

No one really knows what the future holds, but there is an immediate next step you are about to take into it. The moment of planning to take that next step is actually an attempt to look into the future. This can be described as a vision of the future.

Looking ahead with the mind involves a combination of imagination and thinking about what might or could be for the future. Herein lies one of the true secrets of vision – imagining and thinking one small next action at a time then quickly processing the outcomes of that action, and then following on with another action to respond to the outcome and so on.

Exercising and disciplining the faculties of your mind to do this is key to developing vision. It is easier to think about the past because it has happened and you have most of the information about it. But looking at the past only means you have turned backwards and are facing that direction. Someone said, "Create your future from your future, not your past." It is more challenging to look at the future because there is very limited information that we have about it, so, we must exercise the faculty of imagination to play out all the possible outcomes we can think of, to get from where we are now to where we hope to be.

Bringing all this together, I have learnt that having vision is strongly connected to taking responsibility. I can have a vision for my life when I take responsibility for it. My vision grows as I take on more responsibility for an education, job, wife, children, business, community, nation etc.

I have learnt that vision is simply imagining and thinking about what next step I need to take to ensure I do well with my life. What next steps to take to solve problems that limit my family, job, community, nation or generation.

I might not have a great vision that touches the whole world yet, but I do have a great vision that causes me to progress with the things I am responsible for now.

ADVERSITY

"Every adversity, every failure, every heartache carries with it the seed of an equal or greater benefit." – Napoleon Hill

No one likes going through a tough time and we all work hard, hope, pray, wish and dream for an easier life. We all try to run away from adversity and find the easiest way out of a situation, but I have come to realize that, as "necessity is the mother of invention", so it is that adversity has the potential to bring out the innovator in us.

When I was in university, the distance I had to travel to get back home was about 680 miles. I was not as lucky as those whose houses were close to their university. The cost of travelling back home if I needed to was a pretty hefty sum of my budget.

Due to the epileptic nature of industrial action taken by the teaching and support staff in the universities all over the country at that time, the semester would usually stretch out for longer than planned. At those times I had to consider carefully if I should go all the way home, or stay put in case the strike action was called off in less than a week. My decision to stay paid off a couple of times, but there was this instance when the strike dragged on for months. I ran out of all resources and spent my transport money on food. That soon ran out and then the hunger games began. I was a very fussy eater and would not touch certain foods, but after days of not eating meaningfully, my ability to eat anything came out. Once, my room mate boiled grains of corn which were meant for planting, they were as hard as rock and it took about half a day to get a little bit of tenderness in them. Another time, one friend caught a monitor lizard and this was fried and eaten, it tasted like chicken. A pigeon had the unfortunate fate of lodging under the roof outside my bedroom window; well you can imagine what a meal we had. It was a crazy time, but I learnt to survive. In those days I saw that there was more in me than I thought I had. Deep down, I had what it took to keep going in the midst of very adverse conditions. Those experiences, taught me a lot of patience, planning, budgeting, managing and coping with little, and of course how to eat anything.

My experiences over those few months were actually the reality that other people lived through on a day-to-day basis with no sight of an end to it. Some have had it even much worse yet they have become great in spite of the unique and challenging circumstances they had to live through. I always ask myself this question, "If they did not go through those challenges, would they have risen to greatness?" would they have discovered the resilience that they had? Would they have responded to the need around them or even noticed it?

If there was no apartheid in South Africa, would we have known Nelson Mandela and the fight for freedom? If there was no segregation in America, would we have known Rosa Parks or Rev Martin Luther King Jr.? Thomas Edison, known as one of the greatest inventors of our time developed hearing problems at an early age and was partially deaf. In his early years, he only lasted for 3 months in school before being chucked out; he had to sell candy and newspapers on the streets as a child to make ends meet; yet in his adversity he found his ability to turn a profit and also to innovate. If he did not go through what he did, would we have had the benefits of his inventions such as the light bulb?

Adversity as ugly as it can look can be a true helper. William Shakespeare surmises, "Let me embrace thee, sour adversity, for wise men say it is the wisest course".

I have been through many much more challenging circumstances over the years, and as much as I hated having to go through them, deep down, I am thankful for them as the adversity brought out the best in me.

My brother wrote:

"Have you ever looked for the easy way out?

The easy way out is always the hard way in.

So I look for the hard way in and find the easy way out."

– Kayo Opebiyi

I have learnt to stop looking for the easy way out and stand up in the midst of adverse circumstances, to survive, to forge ahead, to let the untapped strength on my inside come out. The effort I spent trying to avoid it, I now use to live through and beyond it.

THE SILENT NOTE

"To everything there is a season, A time for every purpose under heaven: A time to be born, And a time to die… A time to keep silence, And a time to speak… I have seen the God-given task with which the sons of men are to be occupied. He has made everything beautiful in its time…" – **Ecclesiastes 3:1-2, 7, 10-11**

I loved music lessons back in secondary school, not just because the notes looked like tadpoles hanging off a fence made of wires, but also because the teacher was a bit of an eccentric character. He never failed to disappoint, barking out in every single lesson of the term "the order of the scale is tone, tone; semitone! Say it after me, tone, tone; semitone!"

One of the very first symbols I learnt about in a musical manuscript was called a 'semibreve' or 'rest'. This is actually a silent note that usually starts off the musical piece, punctuates it all the way through and then rounds it off at the end. Those playing the overture had to read the silent notes as well as the audible ones. If the instrumentalists or singers failed to observe and play or sing this note, then the music would be out of sync, rhythm and melody.

The importance of the silent note could not be overlooked in the grand scheme of the musical masterpiece.

Silence is not only for music, it is for life, and all through the several phases of our lives we learn to be silent and we learn to speak. As a child, I got told off by the adults, "Don't speak unless you are spoken to!", "Mummy is talking, be quiet!", "Be seen and not heard!" Those instructions were frustrating; because as far as I was concerned I had a lot I wanted to say. As maturity came, I realized that there was wisdom in the rebukes I received to hold my peace until I was allowed to speak.

Sometimes, the wisdom of our thoughts can only shine through after a moment of meaningful silence. Do you know anyone who is a chatterbox? They are nice for a while, but then as they grow on you, all you can think of saying to them is "why don't you just shut up!"

The poem from which we get the saying 'silence is golden' goes something like this "Silence is the element in which great things fashion themselves together; that at length they may emerge, full-formed and majestic, into the daylight of Life, which they are thenceforth to rule… do this thyself, hold thy tongue for one day: on the morrow, how much clearer are thy purposes and duties; … Speech too is great, but not the greatest. As the Swiss Inscription says: Sprecfien ist silbern, Schweigen ist golden (Speech is silvern, Silence is golden); or as I might rather express it: Speech is of Time, Silence is of Eternity." – From Sator Resartus, translated by English poet Thomas Carlyle.

When we are conceived, we do not have a voice for the first 9 months of our existence, we are forming in the dark, playing the silent note, and then we come out loudly, crying and being cried for, fully formed for the next phase of our journey. The first silence is broken, we arrive on the scene and the melody of our life begins. The same principle follows us through as we become the silent apprentices watching the master work, until, it is our time to perform our own tasks. We are the silent student watching the instructor lead, until we become the graduate. We are the silent daughter watching the mother weave the family together, until we become the wife and mother of our own. We are the silent idea that no one knows about, until the work in secret is revealed to the world and then our product precedes us, going places we could only have dreamt about. We learn to withhold action and we learn to take it. We learn that the season and timing of our silence is key to the rendition of the musical masterpiece our lives have become. We learn to prepare for the next great note to be played in that moment of silent rest.

In the 2013 BBC proms, Daniel Barenboim, the world-renowned conductor presiding over Wagner's Ring Cycle, had been faced with a remarkable ten seconds of silence following the orchestra's final note, as an impressed audience sat entirely still. After a rapt silence, more than 5,000 people in the Royal Albert Hall erupted into applause reported to have lasted up to half an hour. The audience had heard the music and they had acknowledged the final note, the silent note; the silence indicating that the piece was done. It was masterfully played, intricately presented and beautifully composed. Silence was all that was needed at that point. When they took in what had just happened, what had just graced their ears, they could not help but respond in thunderous applause and appreciation for music well played.

When my life is lived out and my journey done, when I give my final performance, my best, and I come to a rest offering my final silent note, I would like to think that even though I can't hear it or see it, there would be a thunderous applause, a vast appreciation for what I have done. That it would outlast me for generations to come. I have finished well, I have played masterfully, I have lifted the spirits of my audience and now it is time for those who watched me perform to respond.

MEDITATION FOR EACH DAY

One of the many disciplines of the Christian faith is meditation on the scriptures. In the section following are bible verses that have formed part of my meditation and which I link with each of the lessons learnt.

Day 1 – Joga Bonita

"Hear, my son, and receive my sayings, and the years of your life will be many." – Proverbs 4:10

Day 2 – Joga Bonita 2

"And further, my son, be admonished by these. Of making many books there is no end, and much study is wearisome to the flesh. Let us hear the conclusion of the whole matter: Fear God and keep His commandments, For this is man's all." – Ecclesiastes 12:12-13

Day 3 – Joga Bonita 3

"For rulers are not a terror to good works, but to evil. Do you want to be unafraid of the authority? Do what is good, and you will have praise from the same." – Romans 13:3

Day 4 – Joga Bonita 4

"Then he who had received the five talents went and traded with them, and made another five talents. And likewise he who had received two gained two more also. But he who had received one went and dug in the ground, and hid his lord's money." – Matthew 25:16-18

"Two are better than one, because they have a good reward for their labour." – Ecclesiastes 4:9

Day 5 – Joga Bonita 5

"Do you see a man who excels in his work? He will stand before kings; He will not stand before unknown men." – Proverbs 22:29

"… I have come that they may have life, and that they may have it more abundantly." – John 10:10

Day 6 – Discrimination

"I will praise You, for I am fearfully and wonderfully made; Marvelous are Your works, And that my soul knows very well." – Psalm 139:14

Day 7 – Somebody's Going to Do It – Why not You?

"'If you can?' said Jesus. 'Everything is possible for one who believes.'" – Mark 9:23

Day 8 – The Philosophy of (a) Failure

"For though the righteous fall seven times, they rise again, but the wicked stumble when calamity strikes." – Proverbs 24:16

Day 9 – Keep Learning

"A wise man will hear and increase learning, And a man of understanding will attain wise counsel" – Proverbs 1:5

Day 10 – The Ant

"Go to the ant, you sluggard! Consider her ways and be wise, Which, having no captain, Overseer or ruler, Provides her supplies in the summer, And gathers her food in the harvest." – Proverbs 6:6-8

"There are four things which are little on the earth, But they are exceedingly wise: The ants are a people not strong, Yet they prepare their food in the summer" – Proverbs 31:24-25

Day 11 – Holder, Folder

"I went by the field of the lazy man, And by the vineyard of the man devoid of understanding; And there it was, all overgrown with thorns;… Its stone wall was broken down. When I saw it, I considered it well; I looked on it and received instruction:" - Proverbs 24:30-32

Day 12 – Holder, Folder 2

"Finally, brethren, whatsoever things are true, whatsoever things are honest, whatsoever things are just, whatsoever things are pure, whatsoever things are lovely, whatsoever things are of good report; if there be any virtue, and if there be any praise, think on these things. Those things, which ye have both learned, and received, and heard, and seen in me, do: and the God of peace shall be with you." – Philippians 4:8-9

Day 13 – Holder, Folder 3

"Death and life are in the power of the tongue: and they that love it shall eat the fruit thereof." – Proverbs 18:21

Day 14 – Holder, Folder 4

"And it came to pass, when he had made an end of speaking unto Saul, that the soul of Jonathan was knit with the soul of David, and Jonathan loved him as his own soul." – 1 Samuel 18:1

Day 15 – Holder, Folder 5

"Do you see a man who excels in his work? He will stand before kings; He will not stand before unknown men." – Proverbs 22:29

"Therefore whoever hears these sayings of Mine, and does them, I will liken him to a wise man who built his house on the rock: and the rain descended, the floods came, and the winds blew and beat on that house; and it did not fall, for it was founded on the rock." – Matthew 7:24-25

Day 16 – Holder, Folder 6

"Therefore put on the full armor of God, so that when the day of evil comes, you may be able to stand your ground, and after you have done everything, to stand." – Ephesians 6:13

Day 17 – Holder, Folder 7

"But also for this very reason, giving all diligence, add to your faith virtue, to virtue knowledge, to knowledge self-control, to self-control perseverance, to perseverance godliness, to godliness brotherly kindness, and to brotherly kindness love. For if these things are yours and abound, you will be neither barren nor unfruitful in the knowledge of our Lord Jesus Christ." – 2 Peter 1:5-8

Day 18 – Something for Tomorrow

"Woe to you, O land, when your king is a child, And your princes feast in the morning! Blessed are you, O land, when your king is the son of nobles, And your princes feast at the proper time – For strength and not for drunkenness!" – Ecclesiastes 10:16-17

Day 19 – I Went to Ghana

"And He said to them, "Come aside by yourselves to a deserted place and rest a while." For there were many coming and going, and they did not even have time to eat. So they departed to a deserted place in the boat by themselves." – Mark 6:31-32

Day 20 – I Went to Ghana 2

"And he arose that night and took his two wives, his two female servants, and his eleven sons, and crossed over the ford of Jabbok. He took them, sent them over the brook, and sent over what he had. Then Jacob was left alone; and a Man wrestled with him until the breaking of day." – Genesis 32:22-24

Day 21 – What it Takes to Be a Pioneer

"And Jesus, when He came out, saw a great multitude and was moved with compassion for them, because they were like sheep not having a shepherd. So He began to teach them many things." – Mark 6:34

Day 22 – Responsibility

"And that servant who knew his master's will, and did not prepare himself or do according to his will, shall be beaten with many stripes. But he who did not know, yet committed things deserving of stripes, shall be beaten with few. For everyone to whom much is given, from him much will be required; and to whom much has been committed, of him they will ask the more." – Luke 12:47-48

Day 23 – Money Matters

"Because of laziness the building decays, And through idleness of hands the house leaks. A feast is made for laughter, And wine makes merry; But money answers everything." – Ecclesiastes 10:18-19

Day 24 – The Human Touch

"A friend loves at all times, and a brother is born for a time of adversity." – Proverbs 17:17

Day 25 – Be on Time

"Making the best use of the time, because the days are evil." – Ephesians 5:16

"So teach us to number our days, That we may gain a heart of wisdom." – Psalm 90:12

Day 26 – Discipline

"When He had called the people to Himself, with His disciples also, He said to them, Whoever desires to come after Me, let him deny himself, and take up his cross, and follow Me." – Mark 8:34

Day 27 – Order

"Let all things be done decently and in order." – 1 Corinthians 14:40

Day 28 – Values

"The devil led him up to a high place and showed him in an instant all the kingdoms of the world. And he said to him, "I will give you all their authority and splendor; it has been given to me, and I can give it to anyone I want to. If you worship me, it will all be yours." Jesus answered, "It is written: 'Worship the Lord your God and serve him only.'"" – Luke 4:5-8

Day 29 – Regrets

"Brothers and sisters, I do not consider myself yet to have taken hold of it. But one thing I do: Forgetting what is behind and straining toward what is ahead, I press on toward the goal to win the prize for which God has called me heavenward in Christ Jesus." – Philippians 3:13-14

Day 30 – Forgiveness

"Then Peter came to Him and said, "Lord, how often shall my brother sin against me, and I forgive him? Up to seven times?" Jesus said to him, "I do not say to you, up to seven times, but up to seventy times seven." – Matthew 18:21-22

Day 31 – Be Thankful

"In everything give thanks; for this is the will of God in Christ Jesus for you." – 1 Thessalonians 5:18

"Oh, that men would give thanks to the Lord for His goodness, And for His wonderful works to the children of men!" – Psalms 107:8

Day 32 – Create the Mood

"Why are you cast down, O my soul? And why are you disquieted within me? Hope in God; For I shall yet praise Him, The help of my countenance and my God." – Psalm 42:11

Day 33 – Recapture the Qualities of Your Inner Child

"At that time the disciples came to Jesus, saying, "Who then is greatest in the kingdom of heaven?" Then Jesus called a little child to Him, set him in the midst of them, and said, "Assuredly, I say to you, unless you are converted and become as little children, you will by no means enter the kingdom of heaven. Therefore whoever humbles himself as this little child is the greatest in the kingdom of heaven." – Matthew 18:1-4

Day 34 – I Kept Quiet

"For if you remain completely silent at this time, relief and deliverance will arise for the Jews from another place, but you and your father's house will perish. Yet who knows whether you have come to the kingdom for such a time as this?" – Esther 4:14

Day 35 – Preparation

"The preparations of the heart belong to man, But the answer of the tongue is from the Lord."
– Proverbs 16:1

"Then King David rose to his feet and said, "Hear me, my brethren and my people: I had it in my heart to build a house of rest for the ark of the covenant of the Lord, and for the footstool of our God, and had made preparations to build it."
– 1 Chronicles 28:2

Day 36 – Making Decisions

"And Elijah came to all the people, and said, "How long will you falter between two opinions? If the Lord is God, follow Him; but if Baal, follow him." But the people answered him not a word."
– 1 Kings 18:21

Day 37 – Language and Culture

"And to the Jews I became as a Jew, that I might win Jews; to those who are under the law, as under the law, that I might win those who are under the law; to those who are without law, as without law (not being without law toward God, but under law toward Christ), that I might win those who are without law; to the weak I became as weak, that I might win the weak. I have become all things to all men, that I might by all means save some." – 1 Corinthians 9:20-22

Day 38 – Vision

"Where there is no vision, the people perish: but he that keepeth the law, happy is he."
– Proverbs 29:18

"I will stand my watch and set myself on the rampart, and watch to see what He will say to me, and what I will answer when I am corrected. Then the Lord answered me and said: "Write the vision and make it plain on tablets, that he may run who reads it."" – Habakkuk 2:1-2

Day 39 – Adversity

"My brethren, count it all joy when you fall into various trials, knowing that the testing of your faith produces patience. But let patience have its perfect work, that you may be perfect and complete, lacking nothing." – James 1:2-4

Day 40 – The Silent Note

"To everything there is a season, A time for every purpose under heaven: A time to be born, And a time to die… A time to keep silence, And a time to speak… I have seen the God-given task with which the sons of men are to be occupied. He has made everything beautiful in its time…"
– Ecclesiastes 3:1-2, 7, 10-11

ACKNOWLEDGEMENTS

I am grateful for life and the opportunity to share it with my generation and would therefore like to acknowledge the following people who have been a part of my journey through it.

To my late dad Albert Olufemi Opebiyi and to my mom Yvonne Lee Opebiyi for all the lessons you taught and for those that by observing I caught.

To my Siblings Kayo, Bukola, Toyin and 'Aunty' Bose, there is nothing more important than family when it works and when it doesn't.

To my parent's in-law, Captain Biodun and Cynthia Lisk-Carew who brought up a very special daughter, a precious gift that I continue to be blessed with.

To my wife and life companion Toyin and our two boisterous boys Elnathan and Ephraim, what would I do with myself if I did not have you guys in my life. Thanks Toyin for being so passionate about sharing these thoughts with your social network when I first wrote them, its great to have you in my corner.

My appreciation goes out to the following for their contribution to the project.

Ade Ajetumobi for delivering the design work to my very tight deadline. Anita Lahanmi for proofreading and making sure my use of English was sound. Bukola Opebiyi (evoq studios) and Sheyi Lisk-Carew for your wonderful photographs.

A big thanks also goes to Dr Temi Odejide and the entire House on the Rock London Family for your encouragement through the 'Be Productive' series of sermons.

REFERENCES

Day 4   Roger Federer earnings in 2014 reference www.forbes.com/sites/ kurtbadenhausen/2014/08/25/roger-federer-leads-2014-list-of-the-worlds-highest-paid-tennis-players/#31e4cb752cec

Donald Trump earnings for speaking engagements reference http://uk.businessinsider.com/donald-trump-makes-a-lot-of-money-for-a-speech-2015-8?r=US&IR=T

Day 18   Medical references on hyponatremia www.nhs.uk

Day 21   History of Dr. Kwameh Nkuruma from the Kwame Nkurumah Museum in Accra, Ghana.

Day 23   History of money references "Money" by Mark F. Dobeck, Euel Elliot, Published by Greenwood Press ©2007

Day 24   Habits of the rich and poor references "Rich Habits: The Daily Success Habits of Wealthy Individuals" by Thomas Corley, Published by Langdon Street Press

Day 26   2008 Financial crisis reference www.economist.com/news/schoolsbrief/21584534-effects-financial-crisis-are-still-being-felt-five-years-article

Day 30   Harvard Health research on forgiveness reference www.health.harvard.edu/press_releases/power_of_forgiveness

Day 36   Reference to quote from book "On Penalties" by Andrew Anthony, Published by Yellow Jersey Press, London

Day 40   Reference to poem from Sartor Resartus www.goodreads.com/search?utf8=✓&q=silence+in+golden+sartor&search_type=quotes

Pictures courtesy of www.evoqstudio.co.uk; and https://stocksnap.io

Word definitions from:
www.dictionary.com
www.dictionary.cambridge.org
www.oxforddictionaries.com
www.wikipedia.org

Quotes searched and verified through the following sites www.brainyquotes.com and www.goodreads.com/quotes

NOTES

NOTES

NOTES

NOTES

NOTES

NOTES

NOTES